# my first
# Baking
# Book

## NOTES

- Standard level spoon and cup measurements are used in all recipes unless otherwise indicated. (Turn to page 12 for more information on accurate measuring.)
- All eggs used in the recipes are large unless otherwise indicated.

Ovens should be preheated to the specified temperature; if using a convection oven, follow the manufacturer's instructions for adjusting the time and the temperature.

This book includes dishes made with nuts and nut derivatives. It is advisable for those with known allergic reactions to nuts and nut derivatives and those who may be potentially vulnerable to these allergies, such as pregnant and nursing mothers, those with a weakened immune system, the elderly, babies, and children, to avoid foods made with nuts. It is also prudent to check the labels of prepared ingredients for the possible inclusion of nut derivatives.

Children should be supervised by an adult at all times when cooking or baking. The tasks that can be performed at a particular age or stage in their development will differ from child to child.

An Hachette UK Company
www.hachette.co.uk

First published in Great Britain in 2007 by Hamlyn, a division of Octopus Publishing Group Ltd, Endeavour House, 189 Shaftesbury Avenue, London WC2H 8JY
www.octopusbooksusa.com

Revised edition published in 2014.

Distributed in the US by Hachette Book Group USA, 237 Park Avenue, New York NY 10017 USA

Distributed in Canada by Canadian Manda Group, 165 Dufferin Street, Toronto, Ontario, Canada M6K 3H6

Becky Johnson asserts the moral right to be identified as the author of this work.

ISBN 978-0-600-62966-5

Printed and bound in China.

10 9 8 7 6 5 4 3 2 1

# my *first* Baking Book

## 50 RECIPES FOR KIDS TO MAKE AND EAT!

### BECKY JOHNSON

# Contents

# Introduction

Whoever said never to work with children or animals has obviously not tried baking with little ones because it is a joy to cook with even the tiniest of tots. Okay, so it may get a little messy, but the results are worth it. Children's energy and enthusiasm for cooking are an inspiration, and any doubts that some of the trickier tasks, such as piping, kneading, or rubbing in, are beyond their young years are often dispelled by displays of earnest concentration, determination, and exuberant completion of the task in hand. That they are then able to eat the results of their labor is invariably met with wonder and joy.

Children like to feel that they contribute to family life. They want to be helpful and do what they see you doing. Baking is one way that they can produce real results, ones that everyone can enjoy and appreciate. My seven-year-old daughter is now genuinely excited by other people's birthdays and she insists on making them a cake. This is always received with rapturous delight, making her rightly proud. This book is full of child-friendly ideas for food that you and your little ones can bake together, and all the recipes have been tested on children. A family baking session is a great way to spend time together. In this book, you'll find ideas for a quick lunch or an afternoon snack to edible Christmas decorations and party treats. Together, you can make the food for a picnic or their lunch bag, delicious gifts for friends and relatives, and irresistible snacks for the cookie jar or cake container.

**ADDITIVE-FREE FOOD** Baking at home also gives control back to us parents over what our children eat. The kids can still enjoy sweet treats but without the long list of additives most of us know little about and worry may

harm their growing bodies. Instead of giving your children a store-bought cake, open their young minds to the wonderful variety of textures, smells, and tastes of home baking. Show them where their food comes from and how they can combine different ingredients to make delicious cookies, cakes, and pastries. With a little encouragement, a lifelong interest in food and cooking may easily be sparked at this tender age.

**BE RELAXED** First baking experiences need to be fun. The recipes in this book are easy and quick. They don't require long attention spans but be prepared to step in if your child is wavering before completing the whole baking sheet of cookies. I found my daughter was always happy to sit and lick out the bowl, or "help" with the dish washing in a sink full of bubbles, while I finished the recipe.

The important thing when cooking with little children is to allow plenty of time—children hate being hurried—and not to worry about the look of the results. It's the time spent creating something together that's important.

**LEARNING IS FUN** Children learn a huge amount from cooking without even realizing it. First, there's the exposure to cookbooks full of recipes. From these, they learn that the written word provides information that can be used to make things. They also see photos of other children doing things that they will then want to try themselves. Second, there's the coordination required to measure out ingredients, to mix, spoon out, beat, and spread. Next, measuring introduces children to the concepts of numbers, size, volume, and accuracy. Finally, there's the chemistry involved in the baking itself—the transforming effect of heat on food.

**ENCOURAGING INDEPENDENCE** Because cooking is an activity that uses all of the senses, it completely absorbs children. It gives them a sense of achievement and confidence as they try new actions by themselves. As they become older and more capable, your children will be able to make their favorite foods by themselves, and developing a familiarity with food and cooking at a young age may give them the confidence to be more creative in the kitchen in later life. We live in an age where many people don't know how to cook, and rely heavily on convenience foods and prepared meals. Encouraging your children to cook for themselves and learn how to transform sets of ingredients into cakes, cookies, and eventually casseroles and roast dinners can only be a good thing for them in adulthood and will hopefully encourage them to pass these skills on to their own children in time.

## SHOPPING FOR INGREDIENTS

Not only do children learn about food and cooking when in the kitchen, but taking them shopping for the ingredients you're going to use is a learning experience, too. Whether they're sitting in the shopping cart, or walking along beside you in the supermarket, involve your children in the food shopping process. Teach them how to locate items along the aisles, get them to help you track down specific ingredients, and explain their uses and their origin if possible. It all helps spark children's interest and may even encourage fussy eaters to try unfamiliar foods once back at home.

## WHAT CAN YOUR CHILD DO?

Children can—and, indeed, like to—help in the kitchen from the time they are old enough to stand on a chair and reach the worktop. Covering their hands with yours and letting them think they are cutting butter or spreading frosting gives them a huge thrill and costs you nothing but patience. Even the smallest child should be able to use a cookie cutter to cut shapes out of dough. Children develop at different rates, but between the ages of three and six you'll find they can wash fruits and vegetables for you, stir ingredients in a bowl, and, under direction, add ingredients to the bowl.

Over sixes will be able to use measuring spoons, measure liquids, and beat ingredients with a wire whisk.

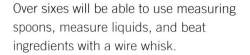 Recipe steps that young children should find particularly easy to carry out are marked with this splash icon. Adult supervision is recommended at all times.

## TIPS FOR KNEADING
**DOUGH** The best part of kneading is that it doesn't really need to be done in any specific way, so you can throw the

dough down on the table and punch it, pull it, and twist it. Children are good at kneading dough, but if they need some directions, tell them to grab the side of the dough nearest to them and, keeping hold of it, push the other side of the dough down and away from them with the palm of their hand. Then lift the far edge up and over into the center. Now, give the dough a one-quarter turn and knead again as before. Do this for at least 10 minutes or until the dough becomes smooth textured, elastic, and no longer sticky. Children can become tired kneading dough, so be prepared to step in and finish the job.

**GETTING STARTED** First, choose your recipe, while keeping in mind the age and ability of your child. Remember that cooking with a little one usually takes much longer than cooking on your own, so make sure to reserve plenty of time to complete the recipe. Collect together all of the necessary ingredients and equipment before you start so that you can check you've got everything you need. Nothing is more infuriating than to have to abandon a recipe halfway through cooking just because you're missing an ingredient you thought you had. It will also cause intense disappointment on the part of your assistant chef.

# WHAT YOU'LL NEED

You don't have to buy any special equipment to bake with your children, but certain items will make life easier.

**STEP-UP STOOL** A child's step-up stool will help your child see above the worktop, or work on a low table.

**APRON** A little apron is a treat for small cooks. A wipe-clean one will make it easy to avoid splashes and keep your little one clean. A cheaper alternative is to use an old shirt.

**SMALL WOODEN SPOON** A child-size wooden spoon makes beating and mixing much easier for little ones.

**SETS OF MEASURING CUPS AND SPOONS** These are useful for accurately measuring ingredients. Don't use everyday spoons or cups because their sizes vary. Fill the cup or spoon level—a rounded measure will mean there is too much of the ingredient being measured. To measure a dry ingredient, place it in a measuring cup or spoon and level it with the straight edge of a knife or spatula. For brown sugar, press it firmly into the cup or spoon. If butter or another shortening does not come in a wrapper with measurements, measure it like brown sugar.

**A LIQUID MEASURING CUP**
A plastic liquid measuring cup is safer for children. To measure liquids, check the liquid against the mark on the measuring cup at eye level.

**PLASTIC BOWLS** As with the liquid measuring cup, plastic bowls are better than glass or ceramic for children to use, in case of clumsy hands.

**SIFTER OR STRAINER** A sifter is ideal for removing lumps from flour, sugar, and cocoa, but you can use a fine-mesh strainer instead to sift the dry ingredients directly into the bowl.

## SAFETY FIRST

Small children must always be supervised in the kitchen. Teach them basic hygiene rules from an early age, as well as telling them about the potential dangers posed by hot ovens, full saucepans, and sharp knives.

**HYGIENE** Always wash hands before starting to cook and make sure surfaces are clean. Tie back long hair and put on an apron or coverall.

**OVENS AND STOVES** Be specially careful when opening oven doors in front of expectant little ones, and make sure they stand well back so they don't get blasted by hot air. Always use oven mitts. Also be particularly wary of recently turned off but still hot stove-top burners. Use the back burners when working with small children so there's no temptation for them to grab saucepan handles from below to see what's cooking.

**SHARP KNIVES** It's great to involve children in the cleaning-up process—to them it's just as much fun as cooking, and you can establish good working practices from the start. However, make it a rule never to place any sharp knives or food processor blades in the sink, where they can be hidden by bubbles.

Instead, rinse them as you work and then place them back into the knife rack or a drawer immediately afterwards, out of harm's way.

## STORAGE

If you don't eat them all within hours of baking them, most of the cakes and cookies in this book will keep for two to three days in an airtight container, such as a cake container or cookie jar. If you want to prepare in advance or decide you only want to finish half the quantity you have made, unfrosted cakes and uncooked cookie dough can be placed in plastic food storage bags and frozen for up to a month.

# A Piece of Cake

# Lemon sand castles

**MAKES** 6   **PREP TIME** 15 minutes   **COOKING TIME** 20 minutes

**Planted with toothpick flags, these little lemon cakes look like sand castles and even have an authentic "gritty" texture from the cornmeal.**

## Equipment

6 dariole molds (or 6-cup muffin pan)
• nonstick parchment paper • pencil
• scissors • paper towels • large
mixing bowl • wooden spoon • small
mixing bowl • sifter • tablespoon •
baking sheet • knife • cooling rack •
teaspoon • medium mixing bowl

## Ingredients

• 1 stick (½ cup) butter or margarine,
  softened, plus extra for greasing
• ½ cup granulated sugar
• 2 eggs
• 1 cup all-purpose flour
• 1 teaspoon baking powder
• ⅓ cup cornmeal
• grated zest of a lemon
• 2 tablespoons plain yogurt
FOR THE ICING
• 1¾ cups confectioners' sugar,
  sifted
• juice of ½ an unwaxed lemon
• pinch of saffron (strands or
  powdered) soaked in 1 tablespoon
  boiling water
• flags, candies, or cake decorations,
  to decorate

**1** Preheat the oven to 350°F. To line the bottom of the dariole molds, place them on a piece of nonstick parchment paper and let your child draw around them with a pencil. Then, if the little hands have mastered scissors, cut around the circles and place one in the bottom of each mold.

**2** Using paper towels, smear some butter or margarine around the sides of the molds so that the cakes won't stick. If you don't have dariole molds, use a muffin pan and prepare the same way.

**3** After helping you measure the butter or margarine and the sugar into a large mixing bowl, let your child do the mixing with a wooden spoon until really creamy.

**4** Break the eggs into a small bowl and add to the large bowl, one at a time, stirring in well. Finally, sift in the flour and baking powder, add all the other ingredients, and stir together until you have a smooth batter.

**5** Help your child to use a tablespoon to spoon the batter into the prepared pans until they are about two-thirds full.

**6** Place all the molds together on a baking sheet and bake for 20 minutes or until golden on top.

**7** Slide a knife around the edge of the molds to loosen the cakes, transfer to a cooling rack, and let cool.

**8** While the cakes are cooling, your child can mix together the ingredients to make the icing. Drizzle it over the cakes with a teaspoon, then decorate with flags, candies, or cake decorations.

**DRIZZLE THE ICING**
USING A TEASPOON

# Yummy stars

**MAKES** 15  **PREP TIME** 20 minutes  **COOKING TIME** 35 minutes

**Dark, moist gingerbread cut into stars and drizzled with a bright white icing, then decorated with sugar stars or silver candy balls.**

## Equipment

large baking pan, 12 inches square • nonstick parchment paper • pencil • scissors • small saucepan • large mixing bowl • wooden spoon or handheld electric mixer • sifter • spatula • toothpick • star-shape cutter • tablespoon • small mixing bowl • teaspoon

## Ingredients

- 1 tablespoon molasses
- 1¼ sticks (½ cup plus 2 tablespoons) butter or margarine, softened
- ¾ cup·cup firmly packed dark brown sugar
- 1 egg
- 2¼ cups all-purpose flour
- 2¼ teaspoons baking powder
- 2 teaspoons ground ginger
- ⅔ cup plain yogurt

FOR THE ICING

- 1 tablespoon lemon juice (or water)
- 1⅔ cups confectioners' sugar, sifted
- 1 tablespoon warm water
- edible silver and green candy balls, to decorate

**1** Place the baking pan on a sheet of parchment paper and have your child draw around it with a pencil.

**2** Cut out the square and place it in the bottom of the pan. Preheat the oven to 300°F. Put the molasses into a small saucepan and heat gently.

**3** Put the butter and sugar in the large mixing bowl and help your child to beat them together until creamy.

**4** Add the molasses and egg and stir to combine. Sift in the flour, baking powder, and ginger and stir in. Scrape into the prepared pan and bake for 30 minutes or until a toothpick inserted in the middle comes out clean.

**5** Let the cake cool in the pan, then turn out and, using a star cutter, help your child to cut the cake into 15 star shapes. Eat the scraps.

**6** Meanwhile, make the icing by stirring together the ingredients in a small bowl. Drizzle the icing over the stars with a teaspoon and then decorate with silver and green candy balls.

# Rock cakes

contrary to their name, these little
cakes are soft and sweet, but they do
look like rugged rocks.

## Equipment

nonstick parchment paper • scissors
• 2 large baking sheets • large mixing
bowl • sifter • wooden spoon •
tablespoon • cooling rack

## Ingredients

- 1 stick (½ cup) butter, softened
- 1¾ cups all-purpose flour
- 1¾ teaspoons baking powder
- ½ teaspoon ground cinnamon
  (optional)
- grated zest of an orange
- ½ cup demerara sugar or other
  raw sugar, plus extra for sprinkling
- ½ cup mixed dried fruit
  (you can make your own by
  chopping citrus peel, dried
  apricots, and candied cherries)
- 1 egg, beaten
- drop of milk (optional)

**1** Help your child to cut large pieces of the parchment paper to fit the baking sheets while you preheat the oven to 400°F.

**2** Put the butter into a large bowl, sift in the flour, baking powder, and cinnamon, if using, and tell your child to rub the flour and butter together until the butter is all broken up and covered in flour and the mixture resembles bread crumbs.

**3** Add the orange zest, sugar, fruit, and egg and stir it all together with a wooden spoon (this stage is too sticky for hands to manage). Add a little milk if the mixture is too crumbly.

**4** Use a tablespoon to put about 12 untidy mounds of the batter onto the baking sheets.

**5** Sprinkle the tops of the cakes with a little more demerara sugar, then bake for 15–20 minutes or until golden brown on the edges.

**6** Remove from the oven and let cool for 15 minutes on the baking sheets, then transfer to a cooling rack.

# Blueberry muffins

**MAKES** 12   **PREP TIME** 15 minutes   **COOKING TIME** 20 minutes

Quick and easy, these ingredients could be measured, placed in two separate bowls the night before, then put together and baked for a special breakfast—a Mother's Day treat perhaps.

## Equipment

12 paper muffin liners • 12-cup muffin pan • 2 large mixing bowls • sifter • wooden spoon • tablespoon • cooling rack

## Ingredients

- 1⅔ cups all-purpose flour
- ½ teaspoon baking soda
- 1½ teaspoons baking powder
- ½ cup firmly packed light brown sugar, plus extra for sprinkling
- 1 stick (½ cup) butter, melted
- ½ cup plain yogurt
- ½ cup milk
- 1 egg, beaten
- 1⅓ cups blueberries
- 1 crisp sweet apple, such as Pippin, cored, peeled, and finely diced

**1**  Show your child how to place the paper liners in the muffin pan while you preheat the oven to 400°F.

**2** Divide the ingredients into two large mixing bowls: all the dry ingredients (flour, baking soda, baking powder, and sugar) sifted into one bowl and all the wet (melted butter, yogurt, milk, egg, blueberries, and apple) in another.

**3**  Ask your child to stir the ingredients in their separate bowls until well mixed.

**4** Help your child pour the wet ingredients into the dry. It is important to mix quickly and minimally—as with all muffins, it's best to have a lumpy batter that will be soft and rise instead of a well-mixed one that will not rise and be tough.

**5** Quickly spoon the batter into the prepared liners so that each is about three-quarters full. Have your child sprinkle each with a little more of the sugar. Bake for 20 minutes or until risen and golden.

**6** Remove the muffins from the oven and let them cool a little in the pan before transferring to a cooling rack. Eat warm or cold.

# Lamingtons

**MAKES** 12   **PREP TIME** 20 minutes   **COOKING TIME** 15–20 minutes

As Australian as kangaroos, these coconut-coated sponge cakes taste exceedingly good and are fun and messy to make.

## Equipment

two 9 x 5 x 3-inch loaf pans • nonstick parchment paper • large mixing bowl • wooden spoon, fork, or handheld electric mixer • sifter • tablespoon • cooling rack • medium mixing bowl • small bowl • saucer • large serrated knife • spatula • board or plate

## Ingredients

- 1 stick (½ cup) butter or margarine, softened, plus extra for greasing
- ½ cup granulated sugar
- 2 eggs
- 1⅔ cups all-purpose flour
- 1½ teaspoons baking powder
- 1 teaspoon vanilla extract
- about 3 tablespoons milk
- ¼ cup raspberry or strawberry preserves

FOR THE FROSTING
- 4 tablespoons butter or margarine, softened
- 1¼ cups confectioners' sugar, sifted
- 1 tablespoon unsweetened cocoa powder
- 2–3 tablespoons preboiled water
- ⅔–1 cup dried coconut
- 1–2 tablespoons milk (optional)

1 Preheat the oven to 350°F, and grease and line the loaf pans with nonstick parchment paper.

2 Put the butter and sugar in a large mixing bowl and, using a wooden spoon, fork, or electric beater, mash them together until light and creamy.

3 Beat in the eggs one at a time. Sift in the flour and baking powder, add the vanilla extract and just enough milk to combine to a soft dropping consistency, and mix together.

4 Spoon into the prepared pans and smooth the top. Bake for 15–20 minutes or until golden brown and springy to the touch. Remove from the pan and cool on a cooling rack.

5  Meanwhile, make the frosting. Beat the butter and sugar together in a medium mixing bowl until light and creamy. In a separate small bowl, mix the cocoa and preboiled warm water together and then add to the butter mixture and beat until smooth.

6 Put the dried coconut into a saucer. Slice the cakes in half crosswise through the middle and spread the bottoms with the preserves. Replace the tops and cut each cake into six equal squares.

7 Dip all sides of the squares first into the chocolate frosting and then into the coconut. Set onto a board or plate to dry completely before serving (if toward the end the frosting becomes too thick, simply thin it down with a spoonful or two of milk).

# Banana muffins

**MAKES** 6   **PREP TIME** 15 minutes   **COOKING TIME** 25–30 minutes

**A great recipe for little ones to make because the secret to a good muffin is not to mix it too well. Lumpy is good!**

## Equipment

6 paper muffin liners • 6-cup muffin pan • small saucepan • fork • small mixing bowl • sifter • large mixing bowl • wooden spoon • tablespoon • cooling rack • teaspoon

## Ingredients

- 2 tablespoons butter
- 2 tablespoons honey
- 2 tablespoons milk
- 2 large ripe bananas
- 1¼ cups all-purpose flour
- ½ teaspoon baking soda
- 1¼ teaspoons baking powder

FOR THE ICING

- 1⅓ cups confectioners' sugar
- 1 teaspoon caramel sauce
- 2–3 tablespoons preboiled warm water
- dried banana chips, to decorate

**1** Ask your child to place the paper muffin liners in the pan while you preheat the oven to 350°F.

**2** Put the butter, honey, and milk into the small saucepan and place over low heat until melted.

**3** Show your child how to mash the bananas with a fork in the small bowl. Sift the flour, baking soda, and baking powder into a large bowl and mix in.

**4** Pour the melted butter mixture into the mashed bananas and mix, then add the flour and mix together with a wooden spoon. At this stage, tell your child not to overmix—just a couple of stirs will do or the muffins will be tough and flat.

**5** Without delay, spoon the batter into the muffin liners so that each is about two-thirds full. Bake for 20–25 minutes, until risen and golden.

**6** Remove from the oven and let cool in the pan for 5 minutes, then transfer the muffins in their liners to a cooling rack.

**7** While the muffins are cooling, make the caramel icing. Sift the confectioners' sugar into a bowl, add the caramel sauce, and mix together with enough of the preboiled warm water to make a thick but spoonable icing.

**8** When cool, ask your child to blob the icing on top of each muffin with a teaspoon and let it run. Stick a banana chip to the wet icing to decorate.

**MASH THE BANANAS**
USING A FORK

# Rainbow cupcakes

**MAKES** 24 (or 12)   **PREP TIME** 20 minutes   **COOKING TIME** 10–15 minutes

## These little orange-scented cakes are iced and dipped in colorful candy sprinkles.

### Equipment

24 small cupcake liners or 12 regular cupcake liners • 24- or 12-cup cupcake pan • large mixing bowl • wooden spoon • sifter • teaspoon • cooling rack • medium mixing bowl • tablespoon • saucer

### Ingredients

- 4 tablespoons butter or margarine, softened
- ¼ cup granulated sugar
- grated zest of an unwaxed orange
- few drops of vanilla extract
- 1 egg
- ⅓ cup all-purpose flour
- ¼ teaspoon baking powder

FOR THE ICING
- 1⅓ cups confectioners' sugar
- 2 tablespoons orange juice
- colorful candy sprinkles or other cake decorations, to decorate

**1** Show your child how to place the cake liners in the cupcake pan while you preheat the oven to 350°F.

**2** Put the butter, sugar, orange zest, and vanilla extract into the large mixing bowl and help your child beat them together until creamy.

**3** Add the egg and beat the mixture again, then sift in the flour and baking powder and stir it in. Spoon the batter into the cake liners with a teaspoon so they are three-quarters full.

**4** Bake the cupcakes for 10–15 minutes or until they are risen and golden. Remove from the oven and let cool for a few minutes before transferring to a cooling rack and letting them cool completely.

**5** Meanwhile, make the orange-flavored icing by sifting the confectioners' sugar into a bowl and stirring in the orange juice.

**6** When the cakes are cool, drizzle the icing over them with a teaspoon or dip them into the icing to cover. Pour the sprinkles into a saucer and dip in the iced cakes. Let set.

**PLACE ON A PLATE**
AND LET SET

# Flower cupcakes

**MAKES** 12   **PREP TIME** 10 minutes   **COOKING TIME** 15–20 minutes

## children love to ice and decorate these pretty, light-as-air cakes.

## Equipment

12 paper cupcake liners • 12-cup cupcake pan • food processor (or mixing bowl and wooden spoon) • tablespoon • cooling rack • sharp knife • small bowls for coloring the icing • teaspoons

## Ingredients

- 1 stick (½ cup) butter or margarine, softened
- ⅔ cup granulated sugar
- 2 eggs
- 1 cup all-purpose flour
- 1 teaspoon baking powder
- few drops of vanilla extract
- 2 tablespoons milk

FOR THE ICING

- 1 pound package instant royal icing
- food coloring (optional; one or more colors, as desired)
- sugar or rice paper flowers or other cake decorations, to decorate

**1** Ask your child to place the paper liners in the cupcake pan while you preheat the oven to 350°F.

**2** If you have a food processor, put all the ingredients except the milk into it and mix until smooth, then add the milk, a little at a time, down the funnel of the food processor until you have a batter that is a soft, dropping consistency. Alternatively, follow steps 2–3 of the Lamingtons recipe on page 23 for the manual method.

**3** Help your child to spoon the batter into the paper cupcake liners.

**4** Bake the cakes for 15–20 minutes or until they are golden and springy to the touch. Let cool for a few minutes in the pan, then transfer to a cooling rack. When cool, slice off the pointy tops with a sharp knife.

**5** Make up the royal icing as directed on the package and divide into small bowls, if necessary, one for each choice of color.

**6** To color the royal icing, if desired, first cover any porous work surface with a plastic cloth, or work on a metal draining board. For each color, pour a few drops of food coloring into the lid of the bottle, then ask your child to add the coloring, drop by drop, to a bowl of icing.

**7** Mix the icing well and let your child spoon the icing onto the cakes and decorate to their taste.

# Coconut raspberry cakes

**MAKES** 12   **PREP TIME** 15 minutes   **COOKING TIME** 25 minutes

### These delicious cupcakes are studded with clusters of fresh raspberries.

## Equipment

12 paper cupcake liners • 12-cup cupcake pan • small saucepan • sifter • large mixing bowl • wooden spoon • large liquid measuring cup • cooling rack

## Ingredients

- 1 stick (½ cup) butter
- ⅔ cup all-purpose flour
- ½ teaspoon baking powder
- 1⅔ cups confectioners' sugar
- ¾ cup dried coconut
- 4 egg whites
- 1½ cups fresh raspberries

**1** Show your child how to place the paper liners in the cupcake pan while you preheat the oven to 350°F.

**2** Put the butter into a small saucepan and melt it over a low heat. Meanwhile, help your child to sift the flour, baking powder, and confectioners' sugar into a large mixing bowl, add the coconut, and stir together.

**3** Add the egg whites and stir together, then add the melted butter and stir again until combined into a thick batter.

**4** Transfer the batter to a liquid measuring cup and help your child pour the batter into the prepared cupcake liners, filling each one about halfway full.

**5** Ask your child to place a few raspberries on the top of each cake.

**6** Bake the cakes for 20 minutes or until they are golden and springy to the touch. Remove them from the oven and let cool for a few minutes in the pan before transferring them to a cooling rack.

**PUT A FEW RASPBERRIES** ON TOP OF EACH CAKE

# Mud pies

**MAKES** 12    **PREP TIME** 20 minutes    **COOKING TIME** 20 minutes

**This recipe is a little difficult in that it needs a lot of beating, but it's worth the effort for the rich, gooey mud batter and resulting irresistible pies.**

## Equipment

12 paper muffin liners • 12-cup muffin pan • small saucepan • medium heatproof bowl • wooden spoon • large mixing bowl, preferably with a pouring lip • handheld electric mixer (or food processor with beater attachment) • sifter • large metal spoon • cooling rack • tea strainer, dredger, or small fine-mesh strainer

## Ingredients

- 7 ounces semisweet chocolate, broken into small pieces
- 1¾ sticks (¾ cup plus 2 tablespoons) butter
- 3 eggs
- ⅓ cup granulated sugar
- ¾ cup all-purpose flour
- ¾ teaspoon baking powder
- 2 tablespoons unsweetened cocoa powder or confectioners' sugar, to decorate (optional)

**1** Ask your child to place the paper liners in the muffin pan while you preheat the oven to 325°F.

**2** Add about 2 inches of water to the small saucepan, bring to a boil, then reduce the heat to low so that the water is simmering.

**3** Put the chocolate pieces and butter in the heatproof bowl and place it over the simmering water in the saucepan until melted, then stir together gently.

**4** Put the eggs and sugar in the large mixing bowl and help your child to beat with the electric mixer for a full 5 minutes, until light and foamy. Alternatively, this could be done more easily in a food processor with a beater attachment.

**5** Have your child sift the flour and baking powder into the egg foam. Add the chocolate mixture and show them how to fold them together with a large metal spoon, being careful not to knock all the air out of the batter.

**6** Help your child to pour or spoon the "mud" into the muffin liners so that each is about halfway full, then bake for 15 minutes.

**7** When the mud pies are cooked, remove them from the oven and let cool for 5–10 minutes in the pan before transferring them to a cooling rack.

**8** If you desire, your child can put a tablespoon or so of cocoa powder or confectioners' sugar into a tea strainer, dredger, or fine-mesh strainer and dust the cakes to decorate.

# Chocolate teddies

**MAKES** 12   **PREP TIME** 20 minutes   **COOKING TIME** 10–15 minutes

The easiest one-bowl cupcake batter made with milk and white chocolate chips. We've decorated them as teddies, but let your child use their own decorative ideas.

## Equipment

12 cupcake liners • 12-cup cupcake pan • large mixing bowl • wooden spoon • sifter • tablespoon • cooling rack • medium mixing bowl • fork

## Ingredients

- 1 stick (½ cup) butter, softened
- ½ cup granulated sugar
- few drops of vanilla extract
- 2 eggs
- ¾ cup all-purpose flour
- ¾ teaspoon baking powder
- ¼ cup milk chocolate chips
- ¼ cup white chocolate chips

FOR THE FROSTING

- 1⅔ cups confectioners' sugar
- 2 tablespoons unsweetened cocoa powder
- 4 tablespoons butter, softened
- white and milk chocolate disks, chips, or drops, to decorate

**1** Show your child how to place the paper liners in the cupcake pan while you preheat the oven to 350°F.

**2** Put the butter, sugar, and vanilla extract in the mixing bowl and help your child beat them together until creamy.

**3** Add the eggs and beat the mixture again, then sift in the flour and baking powder and stir it in. Finally, stir in the chocolate chips. Spoon the batter into the cupcake liners with a tablespoon so that they are three-quarters full.

**4** Bake for 10–15 minutes or until risen and golden. Remove from the oven and let cool for a few minutes before transferring to a cooling rack and letting cool completely.

**5** Meanwhile, make the chocolate frosting by sifting the confectioners' sugar and cocoa into a bowl, adding the butter, then beating the ingredients together until smooth.

**6** When the cakes are cool, spread them with the frosting. Use a fork to make the frosting look like fur and then decorate them, making eyes, ears, and a nose.

**USE CHOCOLATE DISKS**
TO MAKE A FACE ON EACH CAKE

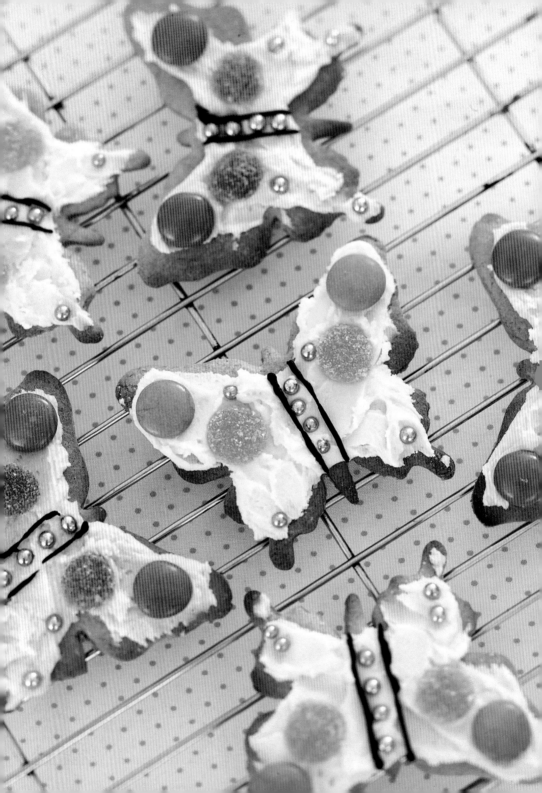

# Cute Cookies

# Chocolate chip cookies

**MAKES** about 24   **PREP TIME** 10 minutes   **COOKING TIME** 10–15 minutes

### These chunky, chocolate chip-laden cookies are quick, easy, and fun to make.

## Equipment

nonstick parchment paper • scissors • 2 large baking sheets • large mixing bowl • handheld electric mixer or wooden spoon • sifter • teaspoon • spatula • cooling rack

## Ingredients

- 1 stick (½ cup) butter or margarine, softened
- ½ cup firmly packed light brown sugar
- 1 egg
- 1 teaspoon vanilla extract
- 1¼ cups all-purpose flour
- 1¼ teaspoons baking powder
- 1 cup rolled oats
- ¼ cup semisweet chocolate chips or milk chocolate chips
- ¼ cup white chocolate chips

**1** Help your child to cut out two large sheets of parchment paper to line the baking sheets while you preheat the oven to 375°F.

**2** Place the butter and sugar in the mixing bowl and help your child beat them together either with an electric mixer or a wooden spoon until creamy.

**3** Add the egg and vanilla extract and mix together again. Sift the flour and baking powder over the mixture and then mix in.

**4** Add the oats and chocolate chips and stir in, then, using a teaspoon and a finger to scrape the dough off, place generous spoonfuls of the dough in 24 or so lumpy piles on the prepared baking sheets. Allow plenty of space between the piles because the cookies will spread as they cook.

**5** Bake the cookies in the ovens on two shelves for about 10 minutes, until the ones on the top shelf are golden brown, then remove them from the oven and move the other baking sheet up from the bottom shelf. Bake them for an additional 3–5 minutes, until they are golden, then remove.

**6** Cool the cookies on the baking sheets for a few minutes before transferring, with a spatula to a cooling rack. The cookies will get crispy as they cool down.

**COOKIES GET MORE CRISPY**
AS THEY COOL DOWN

# Coconut racoons

**MAKES** about 20    **PREP TIME** 15 minutes    **COOKING TIME** 20 minutes

**Disks of coconut macaron with one side dipped in melted chocolate to give them a stripy, racoon look. We like these with vanilla ice cream.**

## Equipment

nonstick parchment paper • scissors • 2 large baking sheets • large mixing bowl • handheld electric mixer or wire whisk • large metal spoon • teaspoon • egg cup • spatula • cooling rack • small heatproof bowl • small saucepan • wooden spoon

## Ingredients

- 3 egg whites
- ½ cup granulated sugar
- 3 cups unsweetened dried coconut
- 4 ounces semisweet chocolate, broken into small pieces, to decorate

**1** Ask your child to cut out two sheets of the parchment paper to line the baking sheets while you preheat the oven to 325°F.

**2** Place the egg whites in a mixing bowl and help your child to use an electric mixer or wire whisk to beat the whites until they form peaks when you turn off (if electric) and lift up the beaters or whisk.

**3** Add about one-third of the sugar and beat it in. Add another third and beat that in, then the final third.

**4** Add the coconut and, using a large metal spoon, show your child how to fold it in gently to avoid knocking the air out of the mixture.

**5** Use a teaspoon to fill an egg cup with the batter, then turn out mounds onto the prepared baking sheets, leaving a little space between each one.

**6** Bake the macarons for 15 minutes or until the tops are golden brown. Let cool on the baking sheets for 2–3 minutes, then remove with a spatula to a cooling rack.

**7** Meanwhile, melt the chocolate by placing it in the heatproof bowl set over a small saucepan of simmering water. When the chocolate has melted, stir, remove the bowl from the pan, and let cool a little.

**8** Help your child to dip the cool macarons into the chocolate and place on fresh pieces of parchment paper until set.

**9** When set, peel the macarons off the paper, using a spatula to help.

**CUT OUT SHAPES**
USING A COOKIE CUTTER

# Sparkly starfish

**MAKES** about 100   **PREP TIME** 30 minutes   **COOKING TIME** 10 minutes

**Buttery shortbread cut into tiny stars and decorated with sparkly sugar, these little cookies make great presents stacked into a cellophane bag and tied with a pretty ribbon.**

## Equipment

nonstick parchment paper • scissors • 2 large baking sheets • mixing bowl • small star or other shape cutter • pastry brush

## Ingredients

- 1¼ cups all-purpose flour, plus extra for dusting
- 3 tablespoons rice flour
- ¼ cup granulated sugar
- 1 stick (½ cup) butter, softened
- few drops of green food coloring
- 1 medium egg, beaten
- 2 tablespoons demerara or other raw sugar or colored sugar cake decorations

**TINY TIP** Rice flour gives the cookies a slightly crunchy texture but can be omitted, in which case use 1 1/3 cups all-purpose flour.

**1** Help your child to cut out two large sheets of parchment paper to line the baking sheets while you preheat the oven to 325°F.

**2**  Place the flour, rice flour, and sugar in the mixing bowl and have your child mix them together with their hand. Add the butter in one or two big lumps and let your child work it into the dry ingredients with their fingers, squashing and kneading it into a soft dough. (See tips on kneading dough on page 10.)

**3**  Add the coloring and squash the dough until the coloring is evenly mixed through and you have a light green dough.

**4**  Dust the work surface with flour and place the dough into the middle. Help your child press out and flatten the dough with the ball of their hand until it is about ¼ inch thick.

**5** Show your child how to use a floured cutter to cut out the shapes, then place them on the prepared baking sheets. Keep squashing the leftover scraps of dough together until you can't cut out any more stars.

**6** Brush the shapes with a little egg and then sprinkle with the demerara sugar or cake decorations. Bake for 10 minutes or until golden around the edges.

**7** Take the cookies out of the oven and let stand on the baking sheets until cool. Store in an airtight container.

# Australian cookies

**MAKES** 16   **PREP TIME** 15 minutes   **COOKING TIME** 20 minutes

**This recipe is based on the Australian and New Zealand Anzac cookies made to commemorate soldiers who gave their lives in both world wars.**

## Equipment

2 large baking sheets • large saucepan • small bowl or ramekin • teaspoon • wooden spoon • large mixing bowl • spatula • cooling rack

## Ingredients

- cooking oil, for greasing
- 1¼ sticks (½ cup plus 2 tablespoons) butter
- 1 tablespoon light corn syrup
- 1 tablespoon boiling water
- 1 teaspoon baking soda
- 1 cup rolled oats
- ¾ cup all-purpose flour
- ¾ cup unsweetened dried coconut
- ½ cup firmly packed light brown sugar

**1** Sprinkle a few drops of cooking oil on each of the baking sheets and have your little one smear it all over with their fingers. Preheat the oven to 325°F.

**2** Put the butter and syrup into the saucepan and heat gently. Put the boiling water into a small bowl or ramekin and have your child add the baking soda and stir it in with a teaspoon. Add this to the syrup, stir, and watch it fizz.

**3** Place all the remaining ingredients in a large bowl and let your child mix them together with their hands, then transfer the dough to the saucepan and stir well to combine.

**4** Show your child how to pile small spoonfuls of the dough onto the prepared baking sheets, using the teaspoon, leaving plenty of space between each pile to allow the cookies to spread as they cook.

**5** Bake the cookies for 15 minutes, until golden brown, then remove them from the oven and let cool for 5 minutes on the baking sheets before transferring to a cooling rack with a spatula.

# Monkey nut cookies

**MAKES** 20    **PREP TIME** 20 minutes    **COOKING TIME** 12–15 minutes

## These are filling cookies with a slightly dense, fudgy center and a crispy outside.

### Equipment

nonstick parchment paper • scissors • 2 large baking sheets • large mixing bowl • wooden spoon or handheld electric mixer • sifter • teaspoon • spatula • cooling rack

### Ingredients

- 1 stick (½ cup) butter or margarine, softened
- ⅓ cup smooth peanut butter
- ¾ cup firmly packed light brown sugar
- 1 egg
- 1⅔ cups all-purpose flour
- ¼ teaspoon baking powder
- ¼ teaspoon baking soda

1 Show your child how to cut out two large sheets of the parchment paper to fit the baking sheets while you preheat the oven to 375°F.

2 Put the butter, peanut butter, and sugar into a bowl and help your child beat them together with a wooden spoon or handheld electric mixer until smooth.

3 Crack the egg and have your child carefully break it into the mixture. Stir together.

4 Sift the flour, baking powder, and baking soda over the butter-and-sugar mixture and mix well.

5 Help your child put heaping teaspoonfuls of the dough onto the prepared baking sheets, leaving plenty of space between each pile.

6 Bake the cookies for 12–15 minutes or until they are light golden with firm edges but still have slightly soft centers. Remove them from the oven and, with a spatula, transfer immediately to a cooling rack.

**SMOOTH PEANUT BUTTER**
IS BEST FOR THIS RECIPE

# Gingerbread people

## Let your little one's imagination run riot decorating these figures, from princesses to action heroes.

### Equipment

nonstick parchment paper •
scissors • 2 large baking sheets •
large mixing bowl • wooden spoon
or handheld electric mixer • sifter •
plastic wrap • rolling pin •
gingerbread men and women
cutters • spatula • cooling rack

### Ingredients

- 1 stick (½ cup) butter or
  margarine, softened
- ½ cup granulated sugar
- 1 egg
- few drops of vanilla extract
- 1⅔ cups all-purpse flour,
  plus extra for dusting
- 1½ teaspoons baking powder
- 1 tablespoon ground ginger

TO DECORATE
- small candies
- icing pens
- cake decorations

1 Help your child to cut two large sheets of parchment paper to cover the baking sheets.

2 Put the butter and sugar into a large mixing bowl and beat until creamy.

3 Crack the egg for your child and let them break it carefully into the mixture. Add the vanilla extract and mix again until smooth.

4 Sift the flour, baking powder, and ginger into the mixing bowl, then stir with a wooden spoon to make a soft dough. Have your child put their hands in the bowl and pull all the pieces together into a ball. If the dough is sticky, add a little more flour.

5 Wrap the dough in plastic wrap and chill it in the refrigerator for 1 hour. When chilled, dust a work surface with flour and help your little one roll or press out the dough with their fingers until it is about ¼ inch thick.

6 Preheat the oven to 350°F. Show your child how to use the cutters and place the shapes on the prepared baking sheets, using a spatula.

7 Bake the cookies for 10–15 minutes or until a pale golden color. Transfer to a cooling rack and let cool.

8 When the gingerbread figures have cooled down, decorate them using small candies, icing pens, and cake decorations.

# Smiley face cookies

**MAKES** 20 **PREP TIME** 30 minutes, plus chilling **COOKING TIME** 10–15 minutes

**Much better than the boring store-bought cookies, filled with plenty of gooey jelly.**

## Equipment

nonstick parchment paper • scissors • 2 large baking sheets • large mixing bowl • wooden spoon or handheld electric mixer • sifter • plastic wrap • rolling pin • round cutters • plastic drinking straws • cooling rack • teaspoon

## Ingredients

- 1 stick (½ cup) butter or margarine, softened
- ½ cup granulated sugar
- 1 egg
- few drops of vanilla extract
- 1¾ cups all-purpose flour, plus extra for dusting

FOR THE FILLING
- 3–4 tablespoons raspberry or strawberry jelly

**1** Help your child to cut two large sheets of parchment paper to cover the baking sheets.

**2** Put the butter and sugar into a large mixing bowl and beat together until creamy.

**3** Crack the egg for your child and let them break it carefully into the mixture. Add the vanilla extract and mix again until smooth.

**4** Sift in the flour and stir to make a soft dough. Have your child put their hands in the bowl and pull all the pieces into a ball. If the dough is sticky, add a little more flour.

**5** Wrap the dough in plastic wrap and chill for 1 hour. Preheat the oven to 350°F. Dust a work surface with flour and help your little one roll or press out the dough with their fingers until it is about ¼ inch thick.

**6** Show your child how to use the cutters. Cut two circles for each cookies, then use a straw to cut out the eyes and mouth on half the circles. Place the shapes on the prepared baking sheets.

**7** Bake the cookies for 10–15 minutes or until a pale golden color. Transfer to a cooling rack and let cool.

**8** Take a pair of cookies and spread ½ teaspoon of jelly on the bottom one. Place the other circle with the face on top and sandwich together. Repeat with the remaining cookies.

# Vanilla flowers

**MAKES** 30  **PREP TIME** 30 minutes  **COOKING TIME** 10–15 minutes

Here's a chance for your child to try their hand at piping. Mastering the pastry bag can be a challenge but the process is an exciting one.

## Equipment

nonstick parchment paper • scissors • 2 large baking sheets • large mixing bowl • sifter • wooden spoon • large metal spoon • pastry bag fitted with a ½ inch star tip • knife • cooling rack • spatula

## Ingredients

- 1¾ sticks butter, softened
- few drops of vanilla extract
- ⅓ cup confectioners' sugar
- 1⅓ cups all-purpose flour
- ⅓ cup cornstarch
- cake decorations, to decorate

**1** Show your child how to cut two sheets of parchment paper to fit the baking sheets. Put the butter and vanilla extract into the mixing bowl and help your child to sift in the confectioners' sugar, then cream the ingredients together with the wooden spoon.

**2** Sift in the flour and cornstarch, a little at a time, and fold in with the metal spoon. Fold back the pastry bag so that the top is halfway down the bag. Spoon in the dough and then fold the bag back up and twist it together from the top down to the dough.

**3**  Show your child how to hold on or near the tip with one hand and the twisted bag with the other. As they squeeze the bag, the dough should be forced out. Continue to twist the bag down as dough is piped out.

**4** Pipe the dough onto the prepared baking sheets in little flower shapes. To finish a flower, push the tip down into the piped flower as you stop squeezing. If your little one cannot manage this, help them by cutting the dough with a knife to finish each flower.

**5** While your child is piping the cookies, preheat the oven to 375°F.

**6**  When all the flowers are piped, your child can press a decoration into the center of each one.

**7** Bake the cookies for 10–15 minutes or until they are a pale golden color. Remove from the oven and let cool for a few minutes on the baking sheets before transferring to a cooling rack with a spatula.

# Frangipane wheels

**MAKES** 15  **PREP TIME** 15 minutes  **COOKING TIME** 15 minutes

**These light and crispy pastries are quick to make. They are great as a dessert, too, served with stewed fruit or yogurt.**

## Equipment

nonstick parchment paper • scissors • 2 large baking sheets • rolling pin • tablespoon • tablespoon • sharp knife

## Ingredients

- 12 ounces ready-to-bake puff pastry, thawed if frozen and taken out of the refrigerator 15 minutes before use
- 8 ounces white marzipan
- 2 tablespoons raspberry or strawberry jelly or preserves
- all-purpose flour, confectioners' sugar, and granulated sugar, for dusting

**1** Have your child dust the work surface with a little all-purpose flour while you preheat the oven to 350°F. Help them to cut a piece of parchment paper to line each baking sheet.

**2** Unroll the pastry onto the flour-dusted work surface and pat it down gently with your fingertips. Alongside the pastry, dust the work surface with confectioners' sugar and help your child roll out the marzipan to the same size as the pastry rectangle.

**3** Place the marzipan on top of the pastry. Dollop the jelly or preserves into the middle of the marzipan and spread it thinly all over with a tablespoon.

**4** Roll up the pastry and marzipan together to make a long log shape.

**5** Using a sharp knife, cut the roll into ½-inch slices. Help your child place each pastry slice on the prepared baking sheets.

**6** Bake the pastries for 15 minutes or until puffed and golden. Transfer to a cooling rack.

**7** Let your child sprinkle the pastries with granulated sugar while still warm.

# Smarty pants

**MAKES** 20 **PREP TIME** 20 minutes, plus chilling **COOKING TIME** 10–15 minutes

## Make a template for these cute cookies by drawing a simple pants shape on thin cardboard, then help your child to cut around the shape.

### Equipment

nonstick parchment paper • scissors • 2 large baking sheets • large mixing bowl • wooden spoon or handheld electric mixer • sifter • plastic wrap • rolling pin • pants-shape template and sharp knife (or cutter) • cooling rack

### Ingredients

- 1 stick (½ cup) butter or margarine, softened
- ½ cup granulated sugar
- 1 egg
- few drops of vanilla extract
- 1⅔ cups all-purpose flour, plus extra for dusting
- 1½ teaspoons baking powder
- 3 tablespoons unsweetened cocoa powder
- package of small sugar-coated chocolate candies, to decorate

**1** Help your child to cut two large sheets of parchment paper to cover the baking sheets while you preheat the oven to 350°F.

**2** Help your child to put the butter and sugar into a large mixing bowl and beat together until creamy.

**3** Crack the egg for your child and let them break it carefully into the mixture. Add the vanilla extract and mix again until smooth.

**4** Sift in the flour, baking powder, and cocoa powder, then stir to make a soft dough. Have your little one put their hands in the bowl and pull all the pieces together into a ball. If the dough is sticky, add a little more flour.

**5** Wrap the dough in plastic wrap and chill in the refrigerator for 1 hour.

**6** Dust a work surface with flour and help your little one roll or press out the dough with their fingers until it is about ¼ inch thick.

**7** Help them cut around the template and place the pants shape on the prepared baking sheets.

**8** Show your child how to press a few candies into each cookie.

**9** Bake the cookies for 10–15 minutes or until a pale golden color. Transfer to a cooling rack and let cool.

**CAREFULLY CUT OUT**
PANTS TEMPLATE

# Butterfly cookies

**MAKES** 20 **PREP TIME** 30 minutes, plus chilling **COOKING TIME** 10–15 minutes

### Here's a chance for your child's creative imagination to get some exercise.

## Equipment

sifter • large mixing bowl • wooden spoon • liquid measuring cup or small bowl • fork • plastic wrap • nonstick parchment paper • scissors • 2 large baking sheets • rolling pin • butterfly-shape cutter • cooling rack • small bowl • handheld electric mixer (optional) • teaspoon

## Ingredients

- 2¼ cups all-purpose flour, plus extra for dusting
- 2¼ teaspoons baking powder
- 1 tablespoon ground cinnamon (optional)
- ½ cup firmly packed light brown sugar
- 6 tablespoons butter, cut into pieces
- 1 egg
- 2 tablespoons light corn syrup

FOR THE FROSTING
- 4 tablespoons butter, softened
- 1¼ cups confectioners' sugar
- 2 teaspoons milk
- few drops of food coloring (optional)

TO DECORATE
- cake decorations or small candies
- icing pens

**1** Sift the flour, baking powder, and cinnamon, if using, into a large mixing bowl. Stir in the sugar.

**2** Add the butter pieces. Show your child how to rub the mixture together with their fingertips until it resembles bread crumbs.

**3** Crack the egg and have your child carefully break it into the measuring cup or small bowl. Add the syrup and let them beat it with a fork. Add to the flour mix and stir into a ball. Wrap the dough in plastic wrap and chill for 1 hour.

**4** Meanwhile, preheat the oven to 340°F. Help your child to cut two large sheets of the parchment paper to line the baking sheets.

**5** Sprinkle some flour on the work surface and place the chilled dough in the middle. Help your child to roll or press out the dough to a thickness of ¼ inch.

**6** Show your child how to use a butterfly-shape cutter to cut out about 20 cookies.

**7** Bake the cookies for 10–15 minutes or until golden brown around the edges, then remove from the oven. Let cool on the baking sheets for a few minutes, then transfer to the cooling rack to cool completely.

**8** Meanwhile, make the frosting by mixing all of the ingredients together in a small bowl with a wooden spoon or handheld electric mixer.

**9** Use a teaspoon to spread the frosting over the cool cookies. Decorate by pressing in small candies and/or cake decorations and drawing with the icing pens.

**CUT OUT BUTTERFLIES**
USING A COOKIE CUTTER

**BEAT THE MIXTURE**
WITH A WOODEN SPOON

# Soft blueberry cookies

**MAKES** 12 **PREP TIME** 15 minutes **COOKING TIME** 12–15 minutes

These cookies are soft, scrumptious, and full of those oh-so-good-for-you-but-still-completely-delicious blueberries.

## Equipment

nonstick parchment paper • scissors • 2 large baking sheets • large mixing bowl • handheld electric mixer or wooden spoon • sifter • tablespoon • cooling rack • spatula

## Ingredients

- 6 tablespoons butter or margarine, softened
- ½ cup firmly packed light brown sugar
- 1 egg
- 1 teaspoon vanilla extract
- 1⅓ cups all-purpose flour
- 1¼ teaspoons baking powder
- grated zest of an unwaxed lemon
- 1 cup blueberries

**1** Show your little one how to cut out two large sheets of the parchment paper to line the baking sheets while you preheat the oven to 350ºF.

**2** Put the butter and sugar into the mixing bowl and help your child beat them together until creamy either with a handheld electric mixer or a wooden spoon.

**3** Add the egg and vanilla extract and beat again, then sift the flour and baking powder over the mixture. Finally, add the lemon zest and mix together.

**4** Show your child how to place tablespoonfuls of the dough on the prepared baking sheets, then use the back of the spoon to spread the mounds into circles. Leave plenty of space between the circles to allow the cookies to spread when cooking. Place five or six blueberries on top of each cookie.

**5** Bake the cookies for 12–15 minutes, until a pale golden color, then remove from the oven and let cool for a few minutes before transferring to a cooling rack with a spatula to cool and become crisp.

# Easy as ABC

# Chocolate scribble cake

**MAKES** 9 squares   **PREP TIME** 20 minutes   **COOKING TIME** 25 minutes

A really quick and easy chocolate brownie-style sponge cake mixture, which is decorated with icing scribbles.

## Equipment

shallow cake pan, 8 inches square • nonstick parchment paper • pencil • scissors • small heatproof bowl • small saucepan • large mixing bowl • sifter • wooden spoon or electric mixer • spatula • knife

## Ingredients

- 4 tablespoons butter or margarine
- 2 ounces semisweet chocolate, broken into small pieces
- 2 eggs
- ¾ cup firmly packed light brown sugar
- ⅓ cup all-purpose flour
- ½ teaspoon baking powder
- icing pens, to decorate

**1** Preheat the oven to 350°F. Place the cake pan on a piece of parchment paper and show your child how to draw around it with the pencil and then cut it out. Place the paper in the bottom of the baking pan.

**2** Place the butter and chocolate in a small heatproof bowl. Boil about 2 inches of water in the small saucepan, then reduce the heat to low so the water is simmering.

**3** Place the heatproof bowl containing the chocolate and butter over this simmering water so that it is suspended on the top of the saucepan and the chocolate will melt slowly.

**4** Break the eggs into a large mixing bowl, then add the sugar and sift in the flour and baking powder. Ask your child to stir them together vigorously.

**5** Stir the melted chocolate and butter and carefully pour it into the mixing bowl. Ask your child to stir the mixture until you have a smooth chocolate goo.

**6** Pour the batter into the pan, using the spatula to scrape as much as possible from the bowl, then place on the top shelf of the preheated oven for 20 minutes or until just firm when you touch it gently in the middle of the top.

**7** Let the cake cool in the pan and then cut it into nine squares in the pan.

**8** Ask your child to decorate the squares with icing pens, perhaps drawing pictures of each family member on that person's piece of cake.

**STIR THE CHOCOLATE**
INTO THE MIXTURE

# Queen of hearts' tarts

**MAKES** 12   **PREP TIME** 30 minutes   **COOKING TIME** 15 minutes

**These especially simple tarts will introduce your child to the pleasures of cutting and eating pastry.**

## Equipment

paper towels • 12-cup muffin pan • 3¼-inch plain or fluted round cutter • rolling pin • fork • aluminum foil or parchment paper • pie weights or dried beans • teaspoon • small spatula • cooling rack

## Ingredients

- pat of softened butter or margarine, for greasing
- all-purpose flour, for dusting
- 12 ounces ready-to-use rolled dough pie crust, thawed if frozen
- about ⅓ cup preserves, jelly, or jam (or selection, such as apricot, strawberry, grape, or lemon curd)

**1** Preheat the oven to 425°F. Using a sheet of paper towel, ask your little one to help you smear the butter around each of the cups in the muffin pan so the dough does not stick.

**2** Dust a work surface with flour and unroll the dough so that it lies flat. Show your child how to cut circles in the dough with the pastry cutter. Any leftover dough can be squashed together into a ball, then rolled out again with a rolling pin so additional circles can be cut with the pastry cutter. Place each circle in a cup in the muffin pan and gently press it down.

**3** Use a fork to pierce the bottom of each circle to let out any air. Tear up small pieces of aluminum foil or parchment paper (about 2 inches square). Help your child gently press a piece into each pastry shell, then fill each one with pie weights or dried beans.

**4** Place the shells in the oven for 5 minutes, then take out and remove the weights and foil. Return to the oven for an additional 5 minutes or until the tart shells are golden brown on the edges and just hardened on the bottoms.

**5** Ask your child to help you place teaspoons of preserves, jelly, or jam in each pastry shell until they are two-thirds full.

**6** Put the tarts back in the oven for an additional 5 minutes. Use a small spatula to loosen and remove each tart from its cup and place on a cooling rack. Let cool completely before eating.

SMEAR BUTTER AROUND
THE MUFFIN PAN CUPS

**DECORATE EACH MUFFIN** WITH A BLUEBERRY ON TOP

# Iced blueberry muffins

**MAKES** 12   **PREP TIME** 20 minutes   **COOKING TIME** 20 minutes

**If you enjoy blueberries and white chocolate as much as we do, you'll love these muffins.**

## Equipment

12 paper muffin liners • 12-cup muffin pan • large mixing bowl • 2 wooden spoons • sifter • tablespoon • small saucepan • tablespoon • strainer • small mixing bowl • large serving plate • teaspoon

## Ingredients

- ¾ cup granulated sugar
- 4 tablespoons butter or margarine, softened
- 1 egg
- 1¼ cups all-purpose flour
- 1¼ teaspoons baking powder
- ½ cup milk
- 1 teaspoon vanilla extract
- ¾ cup fresh blueberries
- ¼ cup white chocolate chips

FOR THE ICING

- 3 tablespoons fresh blueberries, plus extra, to decorate
- ¼ cup water
- 1 cup confectioners' sugar

**1**  Preheat the oven to 375ºF and ask your child to place the paper liners in the muffin pan.

**2**  Put the sugar and butter into a large mixing bowl and ask your child to mash them together vigorously with a wooden spoon. Help your child to add the egg by cracking it for them first.

**3** Ask your child to sift the flour and baking powder over the sugar-and-butter mixture and stir it in, but only briefly. Finally, have them add the milk, vanilla extract, blueberries, and white chocolate chips and quickly stir them in, too. Using a tablespoon, get you child to fill the paper muffin liners two-thirds full.

**4** Bake for 15 minutes, then allow the muffins to cool in the pan.

**5** Make the icing by placing a handful of the fresh blueberries in a small saucepan with the water and heat gently on the stove. Mash the blueberries with the back of a wooden spoon until you have a bright purple mush, then remove from the heat and strain through the strainer into a small mixing bowl.

**6**  Sift in the confectioners' sugar and stir together to make a smooth, purple icing.

**7** Place the muffins on a large serving plate and ask your child to drizzle the icing onto the tops of the muffins with a teaspoon. Decorate the iced muffins by pressing a nice fat blueberry onto the top of each one.

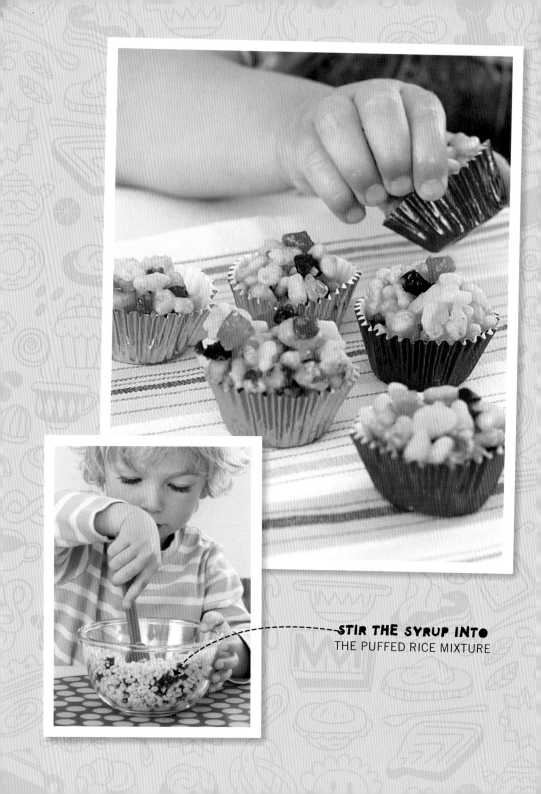

STIR THE SYRUP INTO
THE PUFFED RICE MIXTURE

# Fruity puffed rice cups

**MAKES** 20   **PREP TIME** 15 minutes   **COOKING TIME** 5 minutes

**These crispy rice cups mixed with dried fruits
are perfect for parties.**

## Equipment

scissors • medium mixing bowl •
wooden spoon • small paper cake
liners • large serving plate or tray •
small saucepan • tablespoon •
teaspoon

## Ingredients

- 3 tablespoons dried apricots
- 3⅓ cups puffed rice
- 2 tablespoons strawberry fruit
  flakes or dried cranberries
- 2 tablespoons dried blueberries
  or raisins
- 1 tablespoon light corn syrup
  or honey
- ¼ cup granulated sugar
- 4 tablespoons butter or margarine

**1** Use a clean pair of scissors to cut the dried apricots
into small pieces in a mixing bowl. It will depend on
the age of your child as to whether they will be able
to manage this. Add the puffed rice and dried fruits
and stir them together.

**2**  Ask your child to set out 20 or so small paper liners
on a large serving plate or tray.

**3** Put the syrup or honey, sugar, and butter into a small
saucepan and heat gently until just bubbling. Stir
together, then remove from the heat and let cool for
5 minutes.

**4**  Help your child to pour the cooled syrup over the
puffed rice mixture and stir it all together with a
tablespoon until the rice is covered in the sticky
syrup mix.

**5**  Show your child how to take a heaping teaspoon
of the mixture to fill each liner, but work quickly
because the mixture will set as it cools.

# Polka-dot brownies

**MAKES** 16  **PREP TIME** 20 minutes  **COOKING TIME** 25 minutes

## These fantastically gooey, chewy brownies have polka dots of white chocolate.

### Equipment

cake pan, 8 inches square •
nonstick parchment paper • pencil
• scissors • small heatproof mixing
bowl • small saucepan • large mixing
bowl • wooden spoon • sifter •
spatula • knife

### Ingredients

- 5 ounces semisweet chocolate, broken into small pieces
- ½ cup sunflower, vegetable, or peanut oil
- 1 cup firmly packed light brown sugar
- 2 eggs
- ⅔ cup all-purpose flour
- ½ teaspoon baking powder
- ¼ cup unsweetened cocoa powder
- ¼ cup white chocolate chips

**TINY TIP** If you desire, add pieces of walnuts or pecans to the batter.

**1** Preheat the oven to 350°F. Place the cake pan on a piece of parchment paper and get your child to draw around it with a pencil. Cut out the square and use it to line the cake pan.

**2** Put the chocolate into the small heatproof bowl. Pour about 2 inches of water into the small saucepan, bring to a boil, then reduce the heat to low so that the water is simmering.

**3** Place the bowl with the chocolate over the simmering water so that it is suspended on the top of the saucepan and the chocolate will melt slowly.

**4** Put the oil, sugar, and eggs into the large mixing bowl and ask your child to stir them vigorously with the wooden spoon.

**5** When melted, pour the chocolate into the mixture and stir it in.

**6** Sift the flour, baking powder, and cocoa powder into the mixture. Mix them in and then pour the batter into the prepared pan. Help your child to use the spatula to scrape all the batter out of the bowl.

**7** Ask your child to sprinkle handfuls of the white chocolate chips over the top of the batter in the pan.

**8** Place the pan on the top shelf of the oven and bake for 20 minutes. The brownies should still be slightly soft in the center. Let cool in the pan, then cut into 16 pieces.

# Yummy soft oat bars

**MAKES** 12   **PREP TIME** 15 minutes   **COOKING TIME** 25–30 minutes

### Soft, buttery oat bars made with a splash of apple juice and decorated with chocolate chips.

## Equipment

nonstick parchment paper • pencil • scissors • cake pan, 8 inches square • large saucepan • wooden spoon • sharp knife • spatula • serving plate

## Ingredients

- 1¼ sticks (½ cup plus 2 tablespoons) butter
- ⅓ cup light brown sugar
- ⅓ cup light corn syrup
- ¼ cup apple juice
- 3 cups rolled oats
- ¼ cup white or milk chocolate chips

**1** Preheat the oven to 350°F. Take a piece of parchment paper and lay it on the work surface, then have your child place the cake pan on top and draw around it with a pencil. Cut out the square of parchment paper and use it to line the pan.

**2** Help your child measure and add the butter, sugar, and corn syrup to a large saucepan and then place it on a gentle heat on the stove for them. Stir until the mixture has melted and is just starting to bubble.

**3** Remove the pan from the heat and add the apple juice and oats, then stir together until all the oats are evenly covered. Transfer the dough to the prepared pan and help your child to use the wooden spoon to spread it into all the corners and smooth the surface.

**4**  Ask your child to sprinkle handfuls of the chocolate chips over the dough.

**5** Bake the oat bars for 20–25 minutes or until they are a deep golden color. Be aware that they will still look soft when they are hot but will set as they cool. Remove from the oven and slice into about 12 even pieces but let cool in the pan completely.

**6**  When the oat bars are cool, ask your child to remove them from the pan with the spatula and then place them on a serving plate.

# Crescent moon cookies

**MAKES** 16   **PREP TIME** 30 minutes   **COOKING TIME** 20–25 minutes

## Little almond-flavor soft cookies that are fun to shape.

### Equipment

nonstick parchment paper • scissors • baking sheet • large mixing bowl • wooden spoon or handheld electric mixer • sifter • spatula • cooling rack

### Ingredients

- ¼ cup granulated sugar
- 1 stick (½ cup) butter or margarine, softened
- 1 tablespoon water
- 1 teaspoon almond extract
- 1¼ cups all-purpose flour, plus extra for dusting hands
- ¾ cup ground almonds (almond meal)
- confectioners' sugar, for dusting

1 Show your child how to cut a large sheet of the parchment paper to fit the baking sheet while you preheat the oven to 325°F.

2 Place the sugar and butter in the mixing bowl and get your child to mash them together vigorously with a wooden spoon, or a handheld electric mixer if they can manage one, until they are thoroughly mixed and creamy.

3 Add the water and almond extract and stir in. Finally, sift in the flour and add the ground almonds, then gently stir the mixture together until you have a soft dough.

4 Dip your and your little one's hands in flour to stop the dough from sticking. Pick up walnut-size pieces of the dough and shape into crescents by rolling into logs with fatter middles and curved ends. Place on the prepared baking sheet.

5 Bake the cookies for 20–25 minutes or until they are set and golden. Remove from the oven and let cool on the baking sheet for 10 minutes, then transfer with a spatula to a cooling rack.

6 When the cookies are completely cool, dust them with confectioners' sugar.

**DUST WITH SUGAR**
WHEN COOKIES ARE COOL

**ROLL THE DOUGH**
INTO SMALL BALLS

# Marzipan buttons

**MAKES** 30   **PREP TIME** 45 minutes   **COOKING TIME** 7 minutes

## Little cookies sandwiched with a soft marzipan center and drizzled with chocolate.

### Equipment

nonstick parchment paper • scissors
• 2 baking sheets • large mixing bowl
• handheld electric mixer • sifter •
wooden spoon • knife • small
saucepan • small heatproof bowl •
cooling rack • teaspoon

### Ingredients

• 1¾ sticks (¾ cup plus
  2 tablespoons) butter, softened
• 1 cup firmly packed light
  brown sugar
• 1 egg, beaten
• 1 teaspoon vanilla extract
• 2⅓ cups all-purpose flour,
  plus extra for dusting hands
• 7 ounces marzipan paste
• 4 ounces milk or white chocolate

**1** Ask your child to cut two large sheets of the parchment paper to fit the baking sheets while you preheat the oven to 340°F.

**2** Put the butter and sugar into the mixing bowl. Help your child mix with an electric mixer until the mixture is pale and fluffy. Add the egg and vanilla extract, then beat again. Sift in the flour and stir with a wooden spoon.

**3** Dip your little one's hand in flour to stop the dough from sticking. Show your child how to take walnut-size pieces of the dough, roll them into balls, then place on the baking sheets and flatten slightly into circles.

**4** When there are about 30 dough circles (which should use just over half the dough), cut the marzipan into 30 even pieces and have your child roll these into balls, then put one in the middle of each cookie.

**5** Take slightly smaller amounts of the remaining dough and gently flatten on top of the marzipan to sandwich it and gently press the edges together. Put the baking sheets in the oven and bake for 7 minutes.

**6** Meanwhile, boil some water in the saucepan and set the heatproof bowl on top. Break the chocolate into the bowl and let it to melt slowly, then stir until smooth.

**7** Remove the cookies from the oven and let cool on the baking sheets for a few minutes before transferring to a cooling rack.

**8** Use a teaspoon to drizzle the melted chocolate over the cookies to decorate. Cool before serving.

# Funny faces

**MAKES** 12　**PREP TIME** 20 minutes　**COOKING TIME** 20 minutes

A simple cake batter, like Butterfly cakes
(see page 80), but decorated to make funny faces.
They were a big hit at my daughter's school fair
and caused an excited rush to the cake stall.

## Equipment

12 paper cupcake liners • 12-cup
cupcake pan • large mixing bowl •
wooden spoon or handheld electric
mixer • sifter • tablespoon •
cooling rack • 2 medium mixing
bowls • teaspoon

## Ingredients

- 1 stick (½ cup) butter
  or margarine, softened
- ½ cup granulated sugar
- 2 eggs
- ¾ cup all-purpose flour
- ¾ teaspoon baking powder
- 3 tablespoons unsweetened
  cocoa powder

FOR THE FROSTING

- 6 tablespoons butter, softened
- 1⅓ cups confectioners' sugar, sifted
- 1 tablespoon milk or water
- 2–3 drops of red food coloring and/
  or 2 tablespoons unsweetened
  cocoa powder

TO DECORATE

- icing pens
- white and milk chocolate disks
- cake decorations

**1** Show your child how to place a paper liner in each
of the cups in the cupcake pan while you preheat
the oven to 350°F.

**2** Put the butter and sugar into the mixing bowl and
beat together with the wooden spoon or electric mixer
until smooth and creamy.

**3** Crack the eggs for your child and then have them
break them into the mixture one at a time, being
careful not to let any shell fall in. Beat the mixture
again between egg additions.

**4** Sift the flour, baking powder, and cocoa powder over
the butter-and-sugar mixture, then stir in. Have your
child drop tablespoonfuls of the batter into the
prepared liners.

**5** Bake for 20 minutes or until springy to the touch.

**6** Remove from the oven and let cool in the pan for a
few minutes, then transfer to a cooling rack and let
cool completely.

**7** Meanwhile, prepare the frosting. Put the butter,
sugar, and milk into a mixing bowl and beat together,
then divide into two bowls. Add the coloring to one
and the cocoa powder to the other. Mix in, then let
stand in a cool place.

**8** When the cakes are cool, smooth on the frosting with
the back of a teaspoon, then use your imagination to
decorate them with loads of different funny faces.

**BREAK THE CHOCOLATE**
INTO A HEATPROOF BOWL

# Rocky road bars

**MAKES** 36 **PREP TIME** 15 minutes, plus chilling **COOKING TIME** 5 minutes

**These bars could be made by substituting the marshmallows with nuts (such as pistachios, walnuts, or pecans).**

## Equipment

small saucepan • small heatproof bowl • 9 x 5 x 3-inch loaf pan • nonstick parchment paper • scissors • wooden spoon • plastic wrap • cutting board • sharp knife

## Ingredients

- 4 ounces semisweet chocolate
- 4 ounces white chocolate
- 4 tablespoons butter
- ½ cup water
- 14 graham crackers or plain butter cookies, broken into small pieces (about 1 cup)
- 1 cup miniature marshmallows
- 2 ounces marzipan, chopped into small pieces

**1** Pour about 2 inches of water into the saucepan, bring to a boil, then reduce the heat to low until the water is simmering.

**2** With help from your child, break the chocolate into small pieces and place in the heatproof bowl. Add the butter and ½ cup of water and set the bowl over the simmering water in the saucepan.

**3** While the chocolate melts, help your little one to line the loaf pan by cutting out a piece of parchment paper to fit.

 **4** When the chocolate has melted, let the bowl cool slightly, then have your child carefully stir together the sticky goo.

 **5** Add all the other ingredients and stir again until evenly mixed and coated in chocolate. Transfer to the prepared pan, push into the corners using the wooden spoon, and smooth the top.

**6** Cover the pan with plastic wrap and allow to cool completely before putting in the refrigerator for at least 1 hour until it is set.

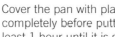 **7** Turn out the loaf onto a cutting board and use a sharp knife and all your strength to cut into bite-size pieces or mini bars.

# Butterfly cakes

**MAKES** 12   **PREP TIME** 20 minutes   **COOKING TIME** 20 minutes

Butterfly cakes, or fairy flips as my daughter calls them, are wonderful children's party treats. An easy, one-bowl mix your kids will love to make.

## Equipment

12 paper cupcake liners • 12-cup cupcake pan • large mixing bowl • wooden spoon or handheld electric mixer • sifter • tablespoon • cooling rack • medium mixing bowl • teaspoon • knife

## Ingredients

- 1 stick (½ cup) butter or margarine, softened
- ½ cup granulated sugar
- 2 drops of vanilla extract
- 2 eggs
- ¾ cup all-purpose flour
- ¾ teaspoon baking powder

FOR THE FROSTING

- 4 tablespoons butter, softened
- 1 cup confectioners' sugar, sifted
- 2–3 drops of food coloring (optional)
- 1 tablespoon milk or water
- confectioners' sugar, for dusting
- icing pens, to decorate (optional)

1 Show your child how to place a paper liner in each of the cups in the cupcake pan while you preheat the oven to 350°F.

2 Put the butter, sugar, and vanilla extract into the large mixing bowl and beat together with the wooden spoon or electric mixer until smooth and creamy.

3 Crack the eggs for your child and let them break them into the mixture one at a time, being careful not to let any shell fall in. Beat the mixture again between egg additions.

4 Sift the flour and baking powder over the butter-and-egg mixture, then stir in. Have your little one drop tablespoonfuls of the batter into the prepared liners.

5 Bake for 20 minutes or until golden and springy to the touch.

6 Remove from the oven and let cool in the pan for a few minutes before transferring to a cooling rack to cool completely.

7 Meanwhile, make the frosting. Put the ingredients in a bowl and beat together, then let stand in a cool place while the cakes are cooling.

8 Using a teaspoon, dig out a circle 1 inch or so in diameter from the top of each cake. Slice the top piece in half.

9 Help your child fill the holes in the cakes with frosting, then gently stick the halved tops into the frosting so they stick up like a butterfly. Dust with confectioners' sugar and/or decorate with icing pens.

# Choc meringue shells

**MAKES** 12　**PREP TIME** 30 minutes　**COOKING TIME** 1½ hours

### Sandwiched together with whipped chantilly cream, these are a crunchy and creamy treat.

## Equipment

nonstick parchment paper • scissors • 2 large baking sheets • large, clean mixing bowl • handheld electric mixer, clean and dry • sifter • large metal spoon • tablespoon • cooling rack • medium mixing bowl • serving plate

## Ingredients

- 4 egg whites
- ¾ cup plus 2 tablespoons granulated sugar
- 3 tablespoons unsweetened cocoa powder

FOR THE FILLING

- 1 cup heavy cream
- 2 drops of vanilla extract
- 1 tablespoon confectioners' sugar, sifted

**TINY TIP** Make sure that the bowl and mixer are scrupulously clean and dry. Even the tiniest speck of oil or water will prevent the egg whites from whisking up to make a perfect stiff and fluffy meringue.

**1** Ask your child to cut out a large sheet of parchment paper to fit each baking sheet while you preheat the oven to 300°F.

**2**  Place the egg whites in the large mixing bowl and help your child to beat these until they are stiff enough that your child can hold the bowl upside down and none will fall out.

**3** Add the sugar in three batches, beating in between each addition. Then sift in the cocoa and fold in with the large metal spoon.

**4**  Show your child how to use the tablespoon and a clean finger to spoon about 12 shell shapes onto each prepared baking sheet.

**5** Bake for 1½ hours until crisp, then let the meringues cool completely on a cooling rack.

**6** Meanwhile, make the chantilly cream by whipping the cream with the vanilla extract and confectioners' sugar until stiff enough to form peaks that stay when you lift out the beaters or whisk.

**7**  Sandwich the meringue shells together using tablespoonfuls of the cream and place in a pile on the serving plate.

# Snack Time

# Pizza faces

**MAKES** 2  **PREP TIME** 15 minutes  **COOKING TIME** 15–20 minutes

It's a strange fact but children will eat almost anything that's been made into a face. I've even seen olives pass my daughter's lips, although I'm sure she'd deny it.

## Equipment

large baking sheet • sifter • large mixing bowl • wooden spoon • rolling pin

## Ingredients

- cooking oil, for greasing
- 1¼ cups all-purpose flour, plus extra for dusting
- 1¼ teaspoons baking powder
- 3 tablespoons cold butter, cut into small pieces
- pinch of salt
- 3–4 tablespoons milk
- 1 tablespoon olive oil

FOR THE TOPPING

- ¼ cup tomato sauce
- strips of bell pepper, olives, cherry tomatoes, sliced mushrooms, basil leaves, ham slices, and pineapple pieces, to garnish
- Freshly shredded mozzarella cheese, for sprinkling, plus slices for eyes, if desired

**1** Sprinkle a few drops of cooking oil on the baking sheet and have your child smear it all over. Preheat the oven to 350ºF.

**2** Sift the flour and baking powder into a large mixing bowl, add the butter and salt, and show your little one how to rub the ingredients together with their fingertips until the butter is broken up and covered with flour and the mixture looks like bread crumbs.

**3** Add the milk and olive oil and mix with a wooden spoon, then put your hands back into the mixture and gently bring it together into a ball of soft dough.

**4** Divide the dough into two and make each into a ball. Spread some flour over the work surface and place one of the balls in the center.

**5** Using the rolling pin, help your child roll the dough out to a circle about 4 inches across. Then lay the circle onto the prepared baking sheet and roll out the other one.

**6** Spoon 2 tablespoons of the tomato sauce over the center of each pizza, then spread out to the edges.

**7** Decorate the pizzas with the toppings. Finally, sprinkle shredded cheese over the top.

**8** Bake for 15–20 minutes, until the edges are golden brown and the cheese melted and golden.

**SPREAD THE TOMATO SAUCE**
WITH THE BACK OF THE SPOON

# Bread monsters

**MAKES** 8  **PREP TIME** 30 minutes, plus rising  **COOKING TIME** 15–20 minutes

**Making bread is easy and a lot of fun. For tiny toddlers, you can make up the dough and let them play with it to their heart's content.**

## Equipment

large baking sheet • sifter • large mixing bowl • wooden spoon • scissors • dish towel • pastry brush • oven mitts • cooling rack

## Ingredients

- cooking oil, for greasing
- 2½ cups white bread flour, plus extra for dusting
- 1 teaspoon salt
- 1 teaspoon active dry yeast (½ an envelope)
- 1 tablespoon vegetable oil
- 1 cup preboiled warm water
- a few dried currants, cut in half, to decorate
- 1 egg, beaten, to glaze

**1** Sprinkle a few drops of cooking oil on the baking sheet and have your child smear it all over with their fingers.

**2** Sift the flour and salt in the mixing bowl and add the yeast, vegetable oil, and water. Mix together with the wooden spoon, then put your hands into the bowl and draw the mixture together into a firm dough.

**3** If the mixture is too dry to come together, add a little more water. If the mixture is too sticky and sticks to your hands, add some more flour.

**4** Sprinkle flour over the work surface and transfer the dough onto it. Have your child knead the dough by pushing, folding, and turning it. You can be brutal with it; the more work, the better. Knead it for at least 5 minutes. (See tips for kneading dough on page 10.)

**5** Break the dough into eight equal pieces and knead into balls. Make a pointy snout at one end of each ball and place on the prepared baking sheet. Leave plenty of space between the rolls because they will double in size. Help your child to make the spikes by snipping into the dough with the tips of scissors. Press halves of currants into the dough for eyes.

**6** Cover the rolls with a clean dish towel. Let rest in a warm place for 1 hour or until doubled in size.

**7** Preheat the oven to 450°F. Brush the rolls with the beaten egg and bake for 15–20 minutes. If the rolls are cooked, they will sound hollow when tapped on the bottom (remember to use oven mitts because they will be hot). Transfer to a cooling rack.

**KNEAD THE DOUGH**
BY PUSHING AND FOLDING IT

**DRAW AROUND A TINY FOOT**
TO MAKE A TEMPLATE

# Cheesy feet

**MAKES** about 9   **PREP TIME** 10–15 minutes   **COOKING TIME** 10 minutes

## Kids will love these really easy cheesy pastries cut into feet shapes and decorated with tiny red bell pepper or cherry tomato "toenails."

### Equipment

nonstick parchment paper • scissors • large baking sheet • foot-shape pastry cutter or foot template (see Tiny Tip below) and knife • cooling rack

### Ingredients

- all-purpose flour, for dusting
- 12 ounces ready-to-bake puff pastry, thawed if frozen and taken out of the refrigerator 15 minutes before use
- ½ red bell pepper or a few cherry tomatoes
- ½ cup freshly grated Parmesan cheese

**1** Preheat the oven to 350°F. Cut out a square of parchment paper to fit a large baking sheet and place on top of the baking sheet.

**2** Sprinkle a little flour onto the work surface and remove the pastry from its wrapping. Carefully unroll the pastry until it is flat, pressing it down gently with your fingers to flatten any creases and mend any cracks.

**3**  Show your child how to use a pastry cutter to cut out about nine feet shapes. Place them spread apart   on the prepared baking sheet. Even very young children will be able to help with this. (If you do not have a foot-shape pastry cutter, see Tiny Tip below for instructions on making a template. Lay  the template on the dough and cut around it with a knife.)

**4** Cut tiny pieces of the bell pepper or tomato, using clean kitchen scissors.

**5**  Sprinkle the feet with the grated cheese, then add the bell pepper or tomato pieces   kids will really enjoy pressing them onto the feet as toenails.

**6** Put the feet in the hot oven, making sure children stand well back, for 10–15 minutes or until golden brown and puffed up. Carefully remove them from the oven and then let cool on a cooling rack before digging in.

**TINY TIP** To make a foot template, get your little one to stand on a piece of cardboard, draw around the outline of their foot, and cut out the shape.

# Mini quiches

**MAKES** 18   **PREP TIME** 45 minutes   **COOKING TIME** 20 minutes

These little quiches are fun to make and can be filled with your child's favorite foods. They are great for lunch bags and picnics, too.

## Equipment

two 12-cup muffin pans • 3¼-inch plain or fluted round cutter • liquid measuring cup or small bowl • fork • small bowl • tablespoon

## Ingredients

- cooking oil, for greasing
- all-purpose flour, for dusting
- 12 ounces ready-to-use rolled dough pie crust, thawed if frozen and taken out of the refrigerator 15 minutes before use
- 2 eggs
- 1 cup milk
- pinch of salt
- 4 slices of ham, diced
- 2 scallions, chopped
- 5 cherry tomatoes, chopped
- ½ cup shredded cheddar cheese

**1** Preheat the oven to 425°F, and sprinkle some oil into the cups of the muffin pans. Ask your child to smear the oil all over the cups.

**2** Sprinkle some flour onto a work surface and unroll the pastry. Have your child flatten it with the balls of their hands.

**3** Show them how to stamp circles out of the pastry with the cutter and place each circle in a cup of the pan, gently pressing it down with their fingertips.

**4** Place the eggs, milk, and salt in a liquid measuring cup or small bowl and beat with a fork.

**5** Put the ham, scallions, and cherry tomatoes into a bowl and mix together. Ask your child to put a tablespoonful of the mixture into each pastry cup.

**6** Pour some of the egg and milk mixture into each cup.

**7** Sprinkle some grated cheese over the top of each mini quiche.

**8** Bake the quiches for 20 minutes or until set and golden. Eat them hot or cold.

**SPOON THE MIXTURE**
INTO EACH PASTRY CUP

# Money bags

**MAKES** 8   **PREP TIME** 30 minutes   **COOKING TIME** 5–10 minutes

**Phyllo pastry is great to paint with a pastry brush and these frilly bags are spectacular and tasty.**

## Equipment

large baking sheet • 2 small bowls • wooden spoon • dish towel • sharp knife • pastry brush • teaspoon

## Ingredients

- ½ cup cooking oil
- 4 ounces feta cheese, chopped into small dice (about ⅔ cup)
- 6 cherry tomatoes, chopped into quarters
- bunch of basil, parsley, or chives, coarsely chopped
- all-purpose flour, for dusting
- 8 ounces phyllo pastry, thawed if frozen
- black pepper

**TINY TIP** Wrap up the leftover phyllo pastry sheets in plastic wrap and keep them in the refrigerator until next time you make money bags.

**1** Sprinkle a few drops of the oil onto the baking sheet and ask your little one to smear it all over with their hands while you preheat the oven to 375°F.

**2** Put the feta, tomatoes, and herbs into a small bowl. Season with black pepper and stir gently together.

**3** Ask your child to sprinkle a little flour over the work surface, then unroll the phyllo pastry onto it. Peel off two sheets and roll up the rest for later, keeping it moist under a damp dish towel. Place one sheet on top of the other and using a sharp knife cut both into six squares, each measuring about 5 inches.

**4** Show your child how to brush these squares with a little oil (pour the oil into a bowl) and then stack three squares on top of one another so that they make a 12-pointed star.

**5** Help them take a heaping teaspoon of the cheese mixture and place it in the middle of the squares.

**6** Now for the difficult part. Pick up the edges of the squares and pinch them together to make a bag. It's easy once you get the hang of it, but very little ones may need help.

**7** Place the bundle on the prepared baking sheet and repeat with the other squares of pastry until you have made four bundles. Then repeat with two more sheets of the pastry until you have used all the filling mixture.

**8** Bake for 5–10 minutes or until crisp and golden, then remove from the oven and let cool on the baking sheet.

PLACE CHEESE MIXTURE
IN THE MIDDLE OF EACH SQUARE

# Garlic puffy bread

**MAKES** one 14-inch circle of bread  **PREP TIME** 45 minutes, plus rising
**COOKING TIME** 10–15 minutes

## children love helping themselves to this wonderful soft focaccia and it's surprisingly easy to make.

### Equipment

small mixing bowl • wooden spoon •
11 x 7-inch shallow baking pan •
paper towels • large mixing bowl •
plastic wrap

### Ingredients

- 1 cup preboiled warm water
- 2 teaspoons active dry yeast
- 1 teaspoon sugar
- 1 tablespoon olive oil
- 2 (6½-ounce) packages
  pizza crust mix
- all-purpose flour, for dusting
- 2 garlic cloves, thinly sliced
- 1 teaspoon salt flakes

**1** Have your child put the warm water, yeast, and sugar into a small mixing bowl. Stir together, then let stand in a warm place for 15 minutes or until frothy on top.

**2** Meanwhile, pour a few drips of olive oil onto the baking pan and have your little one smear it all over with their hands or a piece of paper towel.

**3** Put the pizza crust mix into a large mixing bowl and have your child add the yeast mixture and then stir it all together to make a soft dough.

**4** Sprinkle some flour onto the work surface, place the dough in the middle, then knead it for at least 5 minutes. Let your little one try bashing it about but you will probably have to take over to knead the dough until it is elastic and smooth in texture. (See tips for kneading dough on page 10.)

**5** Place the dough into the prepared baking pan and help your child to press it into the corners. Sprinkle with the garlic slices and the salt.

**6** Smear some oil onto a piece of plastic wrap and lay this over the top of the dough. Let the dough stand in a warm place to rise for about 30 minutes or until it has doubled in height.

**7** Preheat the oven to 425°F. Show your child how to make dimples all over the dough by gently pressing their fingers into it. Drizzle the remainder of the olive oil over it, then bake for 10–15 minutes, until golden brown.

**8** Carefully remove from the oven and let cool for at least 5 minutes before eating.

# Crescent biscuits

**MAKES** about 14    **PREP TIME** 15 minutes    **COOKING TIME** 12–15 minutes

Biscuits are easy and quick to make. They make wonderful snacks—try these spread with cream cheese and ham or warm with butter.

## Equipment

large baking sheet • sifter • large mixing bowl • wooden spoon • rolling pin • 2½-inch) plain round or crescent-shape cutter • pastry brush

## Ingredients

- cooking oil, for greasing
- 1¾ cups all-purpose flour, plus extra for dusting
- 1¾ teaspoons baking powder
- pinch of salt
- 4 tablespoons cold butter, cut into small pieces
- ¾ cup shredded cheddar cheese or your favorite cheese
- ½ cup milk
- 1 egg or 1 yolk, beaten, or milk, to glaze

**1** Sprinkle a few drops of cooking oil on the baking sheet and have your child smear it all over while you preheat the oven to 400°F.

**2** Sift the flour, baking powder, and salt into a large mixing bowl. Add the butter and show your child how to rub the butter and flour together between their thumbs and fingers until the butter is broken up and covered with flour and the mixture resembles fine bread crumbs.

**3** Stir in ½ cup of the cheese, add the milk, and mix with a wooden spoon. Then put your hands back into the mixture and gently bring it together into a ball of soft dough.

**4** Sprinkle flour onto the work surface and tip the dough into the middle. Gently roll the dough out until it is about 1 inch thick (it doesn't need much rolling).

**5** Help your child use the cutter to cut out shapes and place them on the prepared baking sheet. Brush with the beaten egg or some milk and sprinkle with the remaining cheese.

**6** Bake for 12–15 minutes or until firm and golden.

**TINY TIP** To have light, crumbly biscuits, the secret is not to handle the dough anymore than you have to. It's the opposite of bread, which you need to knead.

# Cheesy twists

**MAKES** about 15  **PREP TIME** 15 minutes  **COOKING TIME** 8–12 minutes

### These little cheese straws were my first culinary triumph as a child.

## Equipment

nonstick parchment paper • scissors • 2 baking sheets • cheese grater • large mixing bowl • sifter • wooden spoon • rolling pin • sharp knife

## Ingredients

- 2 ounces cheddar cheese
- ⅔ cup all-purpose flour, plus extra for dusting
- ½ teaspoon baking powder
- ½ teaspoon dry mustard
- 4 tablespoons cold butter, cut into small pieces
- 1 egg

**1** Preheat the oven to 425°F and cut pieces of parchment paper to fit the two baking sheets.

**2** Help your child to shred the cheese into the mixing bowl, then sift the flour, baking powder, and dry mustard over the cheese, showing your child how to use the sifter (or tap the sides or shake a fine-mesh strainer) so the ingredients fall through.

**3** Add the butter to the mixture, then show your little one how to get their hands into the mixture and rub the cheese, butter, and flour together between their thumbs and fingers until the butter is broken up and covered in flour and the mixture looks like fine bread crumbs.

**4** Separate the egg for your child into yolk and white. Add the yolk to the mixture and discard the white. Stir with a wooden spoon until you have a stiff dough.

**5** Sprinkle plenty of flour over a work surface and put the dough in the middle. Children can easily shape this dough with their hands and roll it with a floured rolling pin until it is about ¼ inch thick.

**6** Take a sharp knife and cut the dough into long strips, about 2½ inches thick. Help your child to pick up each strip carefully and twist it gently before laying it on one of the prepared baking sheets.

**7** Bake for 8–12 minutes, until golden brown, then remove from the oven and allow to cool on the baking sheets.

# Sunshine cornbread

**MAKES** 12 squares   **PREP TIME** 15 minutes   **COOKING TIME** 20–25 minutes

A lovely soft, golden yellow bread that's delicious warm or cold with butter. Great with soups, stews, or cheese and relishes.

## Equipment

baking pan, 8 inches square • paper towels • sifter • 2 large mixing bowls • wooden or large metal spoon • fork or wire whisk • toothpick • cooling rack • sharp knife

## Ingredients

- pat of butter or margarine, for greasing
- 1½ cups cornmeal
- 1¾ cups all-purpose flour
- 1 tablepoon baking powder
- 1 teaspoon baking soda
- 1 teaspoon salt
- 1¾ cups plain yogurt
- ½ cup milk
- ¼ cup maple syrup or firmly packed light brown sugar
- 2 eggs
- 4 tablespoons butter, melted

**1** Preheat the oven to 350°F. Let your child smear butter all over the baking pan, using their fingers or a piece of paper towel.

**2** Have them sift the cornmeal, flour, baking powder, baking soda, and salt into a large mixing bowl and mix them together.

**3** Place the yogurt, milk, maple syrup or brown sugar, eggs, and melted butter into another mixing bowl and beat together with a fork or wire whisk.

**4** Pour the dry ingredients into the wet and ask your child to stir them all together, just enough to combine them into a batter, because overmixing can make the cornbread tough.

**5** Help your child to transfer the batter into the prepared pan, then bake the cornbread for 20–25 minutes or until golden brown on top and a toothpick poked into the middle comes out clean.

**6** Let cool a little in the pan, then turn out onto a cooling rack. When cool, cut into 12 squares and serve warm or cold.

# Zucchini muffins

**MAKES** 12   **PREP TIME** 15 minutes   **COOKING TIME** 20–25 minutes

**Delicious snack-time muffins that are especially quick to make and simple enough for children to do all by themselves.**

## Equipment

12 paper muffin liners • 12-cup muffin pan • mixing bowl • sifter • wooden spoon • liquid measuring cup or small bowl • fork • tablespoon • cooling rack

## Ingredients

- 1½ cups shredded zucchini
- 1¾ cups shredded cheddar cheese
- 2 cups all-purpose flour
- 1 teaspoon baking soda
- 2 teaspoons baking powder
- ½ teaspoon salt
- 1 cup milk
- 1 egg
- ¼ cup olive oil

**1** Ask your child to place the paper liners in the muffin pan while you preheat the oven to 375°F.

**2** Put the zucchini and cheese into a large mixing bowl, sift in the flour, baking soda, baking powder, and salt, and mix together.

**3** Put the milk, egg, and olive oil into a liquid measuring cup or small bowl and mix together with a fork. Pour this mixture into the other ingredients and stir until just mixed. Use a tablespoon to spoon the batter into the muffin liners so that each is nearly full.

**4** Bake the muffins for 20–25 minutes or until risen, golden and firm to the touch. Let cool in the pan for at least 10 minutes, then transfer to a cooling rack. Eat hot or cold.

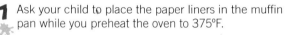

**CLEAN UP ANY SPILLS**
BEFORE YOU BAKE

# Festive Fun

# Little devils' cakes

**MAKES** 12  **PREP TIME** 15 minutes  **COOKING TIME** 10–15 minutes

### These cakes are devilishly chocolaty, with little red horns.

## Equipment

12 paper cupcake liners • 12-cup cupcake pan • large mixing bowl • wooden spoon • sifter • tablespoon • cooling rack • medium mixing bowl • tablespoon • teaspoon or spatula

## Ingredients

- 1 stick (½ cup) butter or margarine, softened
- ½ cup granulated sugar
- few drops of vanilla extract
- 2 eggs
- ¾ cup all-purpose flour
- ¾ teaspoon baking powder
- 3 tablespoons unsweetened cocoa powder
- 2¼ pounds red ready-to-use fondant, to decorate
- 1 tablespoon preboiled warm water

1 Show your child how to place the paper liners in the cupcake pan while you preheat the oven to 350°F.

2 Put the butter, sugar, and vanilla extract into the large mixing bowl and help your child beat them together until creamy.

3 Add the eggs and beat the mixture again, then sift in the flour, baking powder, and cocoa powder and stir them in. Have your child spoon the batter into the cupcake liners with a tablespoon so they are halfway full.

4 Bake for 10–15 minutes or until risen and firm to the touch. Remove from the oven and let cool for a few minutes before transferring to a cooling rack and letting cool completely.

5 Put 1½ pounds of the fondant in a bowl, add about a tablespoon of preboiled warm water, and stir until you have a thick but spreadable icing. When the cakes are cool, spread the icing over the tops with the back of a teaspoon or with a spatula.

6 Have your child take small pieces of the remaining fondant and roll them into devil's horns, then stick them into the wet icing on top of the cakes.

**USE FONDANT**
TO MAKE DEVIL'S HORNS

# Cobweb cookies

**MAKES** 30 **PREP TIME** 30 minutes, plus chilling **COOKING TIME** 8–10 minutes

**These yummy cookies are also known as refrigerator cookies because the dough is chilled until firm enough to slice thinly.**

## Equipment

large mixing bowl • sifter • wooden spoons • plastic wrap or parchment paper • nonstick parchment paper • baking sheet • scissors • sharp knife • cooling rack • small mixing bowl • teaspoon

## Ingredients

- 1¾ sticks (¾ cup plus 2 tablespoons) cold butter, cut into small pieces
- 2¼ cups all-purpose flour, plus extra for dusting
- ¾ cup confectioners' sugar
- 2 teaspoons vanilla extract

FOR THE ICING
- 1 cup confectioners' sugar
- 1 tablespoon preboiled warm water
- black icing pen, to decorate
- small spider candies or cake decorations, to decorate

**1** Put the butter into a large mixing bowl, sift in the flour, and show your little one how to rub the butter into the flour with their fingertips until the mixture resembles fine bread crumbs. Stir in the confectioners' sugar and vanilla extract and have your child squash the mixture together with their hands until it comes together into a ball.

**2** Turn out the dough onto a floured work surface and ask your child to squash it together with their hands and then shape and roll it into a long log shape. Wrap in plastic wrap or parchment paper and chill for at least an hour.

**3** Preheat the oven to 400°F, and ask your child to cut out a sheet of nonstick parchment paper to fit the baking sheet. Remove the plastic wrap or parchment paper from the dough and slice as thinly as possible. Place these slices on the prepared baking sheet.

**4** Bake for 8–10 minutes, or until the cookies are a light golden brown. Let cool for 5 minutes, then transfer to a cooling rack to cool completely.

**5** Meanwhile, to make the icing, sift the confectioners' sugar into a bowl, then add the water and stir it in. Add more water, drop by drop, until you have a thick icing that coats the back of the spoon.

**6** When the cookies are cool, use a teaspoon to coat each with white icing. Use the black icing pen to draw on a simple cobweb design. Draw or stick spiders onto the webs, then let set before serving.

**WRAP UP DOUGH**
TO CHILL FOR AN HOUR

**SHAPE THE FONDANT**
USING YOUR FINGERS

# Pumpkin heads

**MAKES** 12  **PREP TIME** 30 minutes  **COOKING TIME** 10–15 minutes

**children will have loads of fun squashing the fondant for this recipe and rolling the pumpkin heads.**

## Equipment

12 paper cupcake liners • 12-cup cupcake pan • large mixing bowl • wooden spoon • sifter • tablespoon • cooling rack

## Ingredients

- 1 stick (½ cup) butter or margarine, softened
- ½ cup granulated sugar
- few drops of vanilla extract
- 2 eggs
- ¾ cup all-purpose flour
- ¾ teaspoon baking powder

TO DECORATE

- 4 ounces each of ready-to-use colored fondant in red, yellow, and green
- black icing pen

**1** Show your child how to place the paper liners in the cupcake pan while you preheat the oven to 350°F.

**2** Put the butter, sugar, and vanilla extract into the mixing bowl and help your child beat them together until creamy.

**3** Add the eggs and beat the mixture again, then sift in the flour and baking powder and stir it in. Have your child spoon the batter into the cupcake liners with a tablespoon so they are halfway full.

**4** Bake for 10–15 minutes or until risen and golden. Remove from the oven and let cool for a few minutes before transferring to a cooling rack and letting cool completely.

**5** Ask your little one to squash the red and the yellow fondant together with their hands until they are mixed to form orange.

**6** Pinch off a little piece of the green fondant and shape into a ball, then flatten into a circle and gently push onto the top of a cake. Pinch off a bigger piece of the orange fondant and ask your child to roll it into a ball. Place it on top of the green "pumpkin patch." Now pinch a tiny piece of green and roll into a stem and push onto the top of the orange pumpkin. Draw the eyes and crooked smile onto the pumpkin head with a black icing pen.

# Campfire cupcakes

**MAKES** 8 **PREP TIME** 10 minutes **COOKING TIME** 15 minutes

**Simple chocolate orange cakes made by an easy one-batter method and decorated to look like campfires.**

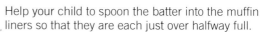

## Equipment

8 paper muffin liners • 8-cup muffin pan • sifter • food processor (or mixing bowl and wooden spoon) • tablespoon •cooling rack • sharp knife • large serving plate • teaspoon

## Ingredients

- 1⅓ cups all-purpose flour
- 1¼ teaspoons baking powder
- ¼ cup unsweetened cocoa powder
- 1 stick (½ cup) butter, softened
- ½ cup granulated sugar
- 2 eggs

FOR THE FROSTING

- 6 tablespoons butter, softened
- 1⅔ cups confectioners' sugar, sifted
- few drops orange or yellow food coloring
- 2 tablespoons orange juice
- 64 finger-shape chocolate cookies, to decorate

**1** Ask your child to place eight paper liners in the muffin pan while you preheat the oven to 350°F.

**2** Sift the flour, baking powder, and cocoa powder into a food processor, add all the other ingredients and process until smooth and evenly mixed. Alternatively, mash together the butter and sugar in a mixing bowl until light and creamy, beat in the eggs one by one, then sift in the flour, baking powder, and cocoa powder and stir until evenly mixed.

**3** Help your child to spoon the batter into the muffin liners so that they are each just over halfway full.

**4** Bake for 15 minutes or until risen and firm to the touch. Remove from the oven and let cool in the pan for 10 minutes before transferring to a cooling rack to cool completely.

**5** Meanwhile, clean the food processor or mixing bowl. Add the frosting ingredients and process for a few seconds or stir until evenly mixed and creamy.

**6** Show your child how to peel the papers from the cool cakes, then take each cake and slice off the part that has risen above the top of the muffin liner. Slice this top part into two pieces and turn the cake upside down on a serving plate so it sits on the cut edge.

**7** Help your child to spread a coating of frosting around the sides and then put a blob on the top of each cake. Stick the two pieces of sliced-off cake back on the top of each cake.

**8** Show your child how to stick about eight chocolate cookies vertically around the sides of each cake so that they look like a stack of campfire wood.

# Hot cross buns

**MAKES** 10 **PREP TIME** 30 minutes, plus rising **COOKING TIME** 15–25 minutes

## Making your own hot cross buns together is a great way to spend an Easter Saturday morning.

### Equipment

2 baking sheets • large mixing bowl •
wooden spoon • dish towel • knife •
pastry brush • cooling rack

### Ingredients

- cooking oil, for greasing
- 2½ cups white bread flour,
  plus extra for dusting
- 1 teaspoon active dry yeast
  (½ an envelope)
- 1 teaspoon salt
- ½ teaspoon allspice
- 1 teaspoon ground cinnamon
- 2 tablespoons candied peel
- 3 tablespoons dried currants
  or raisins
- 1 tablespoon vegetable oil
- 1 cup preboiled warm water
- ⅓ cup milk

TO DECORATE

- 12 ounces ready-to-bake rolled
  dough pie crust, thawed if frozen
  and taken out of the refrigerator
  15 minutes before use
- 1 egg, beaten

**1** Sprinkle a few drops of cooking oil onto the baking sheets and have your child smear it all over with their fingers.

**2** Put the flour, yeast, salt, spices, and dried fruit in the mixing bowl and have your child mix them all together with their hands.

**3** Add the vegetable oil and water and mix everything together with the wooden spoon. Have your child put their hands back into the bowl and draw the mixture together into a firm dough. If the mixture is too dry to come together, add a little more water. If it is too gooey and sticks to your hands, add flour.

**4** Sprinkle flour over the work surface and transfer the dough onto it. Knead the dough for at least 5 minutes. (See tips for kneading dough on page 10.)

**5** Break the dough into ten equal pieces and knead into balls, then place on the prepared baking sheets. Leave plenty of space between the rolls because they will double in size.

**6** Cover the rolls with a clean dish towel, then let stand in a warm place for 1 hour or until doubled in size.

**7** Unroll the pastry and cut into strips ½ inch wide. Have your child brush the buns with the beaten egg and then lay the pastry strips over them to form a cross. Trim the pastry and use the scraps for the next bun until all the buns are decorated.

**8** Brush the buns again with egg and bake in the oven for 15–25 minutes or until golden. Remove from the oven and let cool for a few minutes, then transfer to a cooling rack and let cool or eat warm.

# Easter nests

**MAKES** 12   **PREP TIME** 20 minutes   **COOKING TIME** 20 minutes

## Wonderfully simple, little oaty nests are filled with chocolate eggs for Easter.

### Equipment

12 paper cupcake liners •
12-cup cupcake pan • large
saucepan • wooden spoon •
tablespoon • teaspoon

### Ingredients

- 6 tablespoons butter
- ¼ cup firmly packed light brown sugar
- 1 tablespoon light corn syrup or honey
- 1⅓ cups rolled oats
- mini chocolate eggs, to decorate

1 Preheat the oven to 350°F. Show your assistant chef how to place the paper liners in the cups of the cupcake pan.

2 Help your child to measure the butter, sugar, and corn syrup or honey and add to a large saucepan.

3 Place over gentle heat on the stove and stir until melted together and just starting to bubble. Remove the pan from the heat and add the oats, then stir together until they are evenly covered.

4 Use a tablespoon to spoon the dough into the paper liners so that they are nearly full.

5 Bake for 15 minutes. Remove them from the oven for your child and let cool for 15 minutes, then help them to make a dip in the middle of each one with the tip of a teaspoon so that they look like little nests.

6 Let finish cooling. When the nests are cool, ask your child to put a few mini eggs into each one to decorate, then peel off the paper liners to serve.

**PLACE A FEW EGGS**
IN EACH NEST

**ADD A TAIL**
TO EACH EASTER BUNNY

# Easter cookies

**MAKES** 30  **PREP TIME** 30 minutes, plus chilling  **COOKING TIME** 10–15 minutes

**This dough is quick to make and can be cut into whatever shapes you want, then decorated with imagination.**

## Equipment

nonstick parchment paper • scissors • 2 large baking sheets • large mixing bowl • wooden spoon or handheld electric mixer • sifter • plastic wrap • rolling pin • 1 large and 1 small bunny and/or chick-shape cutters • cooling rack • 2 small mixing bowls • tablespoon • teaspoon

## Ingredients

- 1 stick (½ cup) butter or margarine, softened
- ½ cup granulated sugar
- 1 egg
- few drops of vanilla extract
- 2 cups all-purpose flour, plus extra for dusting

TO DECORATE
- 2 tablespoons preboiled warm water
- 2 cups confectioners' sugar

FOR THE CHICKS
- yellow food coloring
- small cake decorations or icing pens

FOR THE BUNNIES
- few white miniature marshmallows or other bunny tail-like decorations

**1** Help your child to cut two large sheets of parchment paper to cover the baking sheets.

**2** Put the butter and sugar into a large mixing bowl and help your child beat them until creamy with a wooden spoon or handheld electric mixer.

**3** Crack the egg for your child and add with the vanilla extract. Mix again until smooth.

**4** Sift in the flour and stir to make a soft dough. Have your child use their hands to pull all the pieces together into a ball. If the dough is sticky, add a little more flour.

**5** Wrap the dough in plastic wrap and chill it for 1 hour.

**6** Preheat the oven to 350°F. Dust a work surface with flour and help your little one roll or press out the dough with their fingers until it is about ¼ inch thick.

**7** Show your child how to use the cutters to cut out bunnies and chicks and place them on the prepared baking sheets.

**8** Bake the cookies for 10–15 minutes or until a pale golden color, then transfer to a cooling rack and let cool.

**9** To make an icing, stir the warm water into the confectioners' sugar in one bowl. Transfer half the icing to the second bowl. Adding the coloring to one bowl, drop by drop. Use a teaspoon to spread the white icing over the bunnies and the yellow icing over the chicks, then decorate with cake decorations and/or icing pens.

**PLACE CHERRY PIECES**
BETWEEN THE BALLS

# Christmas garlands

**MAKES** 6   **PREP TIME** 30 minutes   **COOKING TIME** 15 minutes

**These garlands are fun to make and very christmassy. Instead of eating them, they could be hung by ribbons from your tree.**

## Equipment

nonstick parchment paper • scissors • 2 baking sheets • large mixing bowl • sifter • wooden spoon • pastry brush • cooling rack

## Ingredients

- 4 tablespoons butter
- 1¼ cups all-purpose flour
- ¼ cup granulated sugar, plus a little extra for sprinkling
- finely grated zest of a small unwaxed lemon
- 1 egg, beaten
- pieces of angelica and candied cherries, to decorate

**1** Help your child to cut out and line two baking sheets with the nonstick paper while you preheat the oven to 375°F.

**2**  Put the butter in a bowl, sift in the flour, and show your child how to rub the ingredients together between their thumbs and fingers until the mixture resembles fine bread crumbs.

**3**  Add the sugar and lemon zest and have your little one stir everything together with a wooden spoon. Add most of the egg and stir again until the mixture comes together, then have them put their hands in again and draw the dough together into a ball.

**4**  Show your child how to pick off small pieces of dough and roll them into balls, each about the size of a cherry. Press eight balls of the cookie dough together into a circle, then repeat to make another five garlands. Place small pieces of candied cherry or angelica between the balls.

**5** Bake for about 15 minutes, until pale golden in color.

**6** Just before the end of the cooking time, brush with the remainder of the egg and sprinkle with granulated sugar, then return to the oven to finish cooking.

**7** Remove from the oven and let cool a little before transferring to a cooling rack.

# Meringue snowmen

**MAKES** 9–12  **PREP TIME** 20 minutes  **COOKING TIME** 1½ hours or overnight

**Meringues are a real favorite of ours and with an electric mixer they're a cinch to make. Children will enjoy making the snowmen shapes and giving them faces and will relish eating them.**

## Equipment

nonstick parchment paper • scissors • 2 baking sheets • small bowl • a clean and dry handheld electric mixer or wire whisk • large clean mixing bowl • teaspoon • tablespoon

## Ingredients

- 3 egg whites
- ⅔ cup granulated sugar

TO DECORATE
- dried currants
- candied cherries, cut into pieces
- candied peel

**1** Preheat the oven to its lowest setting and help your child cut out two squares of nonstick parchment paper to fit the baking sheets.

**2** Show your child how to separate the egg white from the yolk by cracking each egg in half over a bowl and carefully tipping the egg yolk from one half of the shell to the other while letting the white fall into the bowl below.

**3** Help them to beat the egg whites in a mixing bowl with an electric mixer or wire whisk until the egg whites form firm peaks and you can hold the bowl upside down without the mixture falling out. Add half the sugar and briefly beat again, then add the remaining sugar and beat again but only enough to mix in the sugar and make a thick, glossy meringue mixture.

**4** Show your child how to use a teaspoon to place a meringue head on a prepared baking sheet and then use a tablespoon for the snowman's body. Repeat to make 9 to 12 snowmen. Use dried currants for their eyes, candied cherry pieces for their mouths, and give them buttons down their fronts with more dried currants or pieces of candied peel.

**5** Bake the meringues for 1½ hours. For best results, put them in the oven for an hour and then turn it off, leaving the meringues in there for 3–4 hours or until the oven is completely cool. This can easily be done overnight. In the morning, you will have perfectly crisp meringues.

**TINY TIP** To whisk egg whites well, the bowl and beaters or whisk must be scrupulously clean and dry.

**SHOW HIM OFF**
BEFORE YOU EAT HIM UP

**CRUSH THE CORNFLAKES**
WITH A ROLLING PIN

# Rudolph's Santa snacks

**MAKES** about 14    **PREP TIME** 15 minutes    **COOKING TIME** 15 minutes

**We have it on good authority that Rudolph likes to make these to keep Santa going through the most important night of the year.**

## Equipment

nonstick parchment paper • scissors • baking sheet • plastic bag • rolling pin • plate • large mixing bowl • wooden spoon • sifter • cooling rack

## Ingredients

- 2 cups cornflakes
- 1 stick (½ cup) butter or margarine, softened
- ⅓ cup granulated sugar
- 1 egg yolk
- few drops of vanilla extract
- 1 cup all-purpose flour
- 1 teaspoon baking powder
- 3 tablespoons cornstarch
- 7 candied cherries, to decorate

**1** Preheat the oven to 375°F and help your child to cut out a piece of parchment paper to fit the baking sheet.

**2**  Put the cornflakes in a plastic bag and have your little one crush them with their hand or bash them with a rolling pin, then transfer to a plate and keep for later.

**3** Put the butter and sugar into the mixing bowl and help your child cream them together with a wooden spoon until pale and fluffy.

**4**  Add the egg yolk and vanilla extract and stir in. Sift the flour, baking powder, and cornstarch over the butter-and-sugar mixture, then stir them into the mix.

**5** Ask your child to wet their hands so that the dough doesn't stick, then take walnut-size amounts of the dough and roll them into about 14 balls.

**6**  Next, roll the balls in the cornflakes until covered. Place them on the prepared baking sheets, leaving plenty of space between each, and decorate the top of each one with half a candied cherry.

**7** Bake the cookies for 15 minutes or until a light golden brown, then remove from the oven and let cool a little before transferring to a cooling rack.

# Gingerbread house

**MAKES** 1  **PREP TIME** 45 minutes, plus chilling  **COOKING TIME** 15 minutes

**This house is fun to make, but very little ones will need help with the templates and with assembly.**

## Equipment

nonstick parchment paper • scissors • baking sheet • large mixing bowl • wooden spoon or handheld electric mixer • sifter • plastic wrap • pencil • ruler • rolling pin • sharp knife • spatula • small bowl • tablespoon • pastry bag

## Ingredients

- 1 stick (½ cup) butter or margarine, softened
- ½ cup granulated sugar
- 1 egg
- few drops of vanilla extract
- 1⅔ cups all-purpose flour, plus extra for dusting
- 1½ teaspoons baking powder
- 1 tablespoon ground ginger

ICING

- 1 cup confectioners' sugar
- 1 tablespoon preboiled warm water
- icing pens (optional), to decorate
- candies and Christmas cake decorations, to decorate

**1** Help your child to cut a large sheet of parchment paper to cover the baking sheet. Follow steps 2–4 for the Gingerbread People on page 46, then wrap the dough in plastic wrap and chill it for 1 hour.

**2** Meanwhile, make the templates for the houses. Take a large sheet of parchment paper and draw on it one 4 x 6-inch rectangle, two 4 x 3-inch rectangles, and two triangles, each with two sides measuring 2½ inches and one side measuring 2 inches. Cut out these shapes.

**3** Preheat the oven to 350°F. Sprinkle the work surface with flour and roll the dough out so that it is about ¼ inch thick. Place the templates on the dough and cut around them with a sharp knife. Transfer each piece to a baking sheet with a spatula. Bake for 15 minutes, then remove from the oven and let cool on the baking sheet.

**4** To make the icing, sift the confectioners' sugar into a bowl, then stir together with the water until you have a thick consistency.

**5** Spoon the icing into a pastry bag and twist the top together down to the icing, then pipe the icing onto the house.

 Use the largest oblong cookie as the bottom and use the two small oblongs to form a tent shape on top. Secure with plenty of icing along the seam (this will look like fallen snow) and let set. Pipe icing along the edges of the triangles and carefully insert one into each end of the tent to enclose.

**7** Use more icing, or an icing pen, and candies to decorate the house with windows and a door. Let set.

# Index

## ACKNOWLEDGMENTS

CONSULTANT PUBLISHER: Sarah Ford
EDITORIAL ASSISTANT: Meri Pentikäinen
DESIGN: Eoghan O'Brien and Clare Barber
PHOTOGRAPHER: Vanessa Davies
PROPS STYLIST: Marianne De Vries
HOME ECONOMIST: Becky Johnson
PRODUCTION CONTROLLER: Sarah-Jayne Johnson

Huge thank yous from the author to her mom,
Sally Johnson, for introducing her to the pleasures
of baking and for her enduring support and to her
daughter, Summer, for her enthusiastic recipe testing
and tasting. Also to Marcus, Tash, Leo, and Lara for
all their generous help during the writing process.